T0154457

THE ROYAL COURT THEATRE PRESE
PRODUCED IN ASSOCIATION WITH L

ear for eye

by debbie tucker green

ear for eye was first performed at the Royal Court Jerwood
Theatre Downstairs, Sloane Square, on Thursday 25 October 2018.

ear for eye

by debbie tucker green

CAST (in alphabetical order)

Son (UK) **Jamal Ajala**
Young Adult (US) **Tosin Cole**
Friend 1 **Seroca Davis**
Dad (UK) **George Eggay**
Male (Part 2) (US) **Demetri Goritsas**
Woman (UK) **Michelle Greenidge**
Man (UK) **Eric Kofi Abrefa**
Female (Part 2) (US) **Lashana Lynch**
Son (US) **Hayden McLean**
Young Woman (US) **Kayla Meikle**
Friend 2 **Shaniqua Okwok**
Adult (US) **Nicholas Pinnock**
Mom (US) **Sarah Quist**
Mum (UK) **Anita Reynolds**
Dad (US) **Faz Singhateh**
Older Woman **Angela Wynter**

ear for eye

by debbie tucker green

Writer/Director **debbie tucker green**
Designer **Merle Hensel**
Lighting Designer **Paule Constable**
Sound Designer **Christopher Shutt**
Movement Director **Vicki Manderson**
Assistant Director **Anthony Simpson-Pike**
Casting Director **Amy Ball**
Costume Supervisor **Lucy Walshaw**
Production Manager **Marius Rønning**
Stage Manager **Lizzie Chapman**
Deputy Stage Manager **Charlotte Padgham**
Assistant Stage Manager **Sayeedah Supersad**
Deaf Consultant **Deepa Shastri**
BSL interpreters **Chris Curran, Sula Gleeson, Naomi Gray, Anna Kitson, Alison Pottinger, Beverley Wilson**
Dialect Coach **Hazel Holder**
Music Director **Michael Henry**
Set built by **Ridiculous Solutions**

The Royal Court & Stage Management wish to thank the following for their help with this production:
Roger Graham from Digital 4, Lorna Heap.

ear for eye
by debbie tucker green

Film Production
Writer/Director **debbie tucker green**
Producer **Fiona Lamptey**
Director of Photography **Joel Honeywell**
Editor **Mdhamiri á Nkemi**
Colourist **Joseph Bicknell at CHEAT**
Sound Mix **Daniel Jaramillo at SoundNode**
UK Casting **Aisha Walters (Aisha Bywaters Casting)**
Casting Assistant **Ceri Larcombe**
US Casting **David Caparelliotis (Caparelliotis Casting)**
Casting Assistant **Lauren Port**
Casting Associate **Joseph Gery**
ARRI Executive **Simon Surtees**

UK Unit
1st Assistant Director **Yasmin Godo**
A Camera Focus Puller **Kate Molins**
B Camera Operator **Phoebe Arnstein**
B Camera Focus Puller **Eve Carreño**
Camera Assistant **Cristina Cretu**
Gaffer **Max Gregory**
Junior Production Manager **Jessica Cobham-Dineen**
Location Sound Recordist **Johan Winstedt**
DIT **John Miguel King, Sophie Baggaley**
Auto Cue **Louisa Swiergon**
Studio Manager **Peter Gregory**
Production Assistant **Daniella Artry**
Makeup **Tytti Vaaleri**
Makeup Assistant **Katie Wallis**

US Unit
1st Assistant Director **Kenny Lozyniak**
A Camera Focus Puller **Jack Berner**
B Camera Operator **Rachel Batashvili**
B Camera Focus Puller **Alexandra Bock**
Camera Assistant **Josh Reyes**
Gaffer **Alan Mohammed**
Location Sound Recordist **Tim Race**
Data Manager **Hunter Fairstone**
Auto Cue **Evan Torrens (c/o Telescript)**
Studio Manager **Tracy Donovan**
Production Assistant **Edwin De Jesus**
Makeup **Tetiana Glushchenko**
Makeup Assistant **Christopher Barton**

ear for eye
by debbie tucker green

debbie tucker green
(Writer/Director)

For the Royal Court: **a profoundly affectionate, passionate devotion to someone *(-noun)*, hang, truth & reconciliation, random, stoning mary.**

Other theatre includes: **nut (National); generations (Young Vic); trade (RSC/RSC at Soho); born bad (Hampstead); dirty butterfly (Soho).**

Film & television includes: **swirl, second coming, random.**

Radio includes: **Assata Shakur – The FBI's Most Wanted Woman [adaptation], lament, gone, random, handprint, freefall.**

Directing includes: **a profoundly affectionate, passionate devotion to someone *(-noun)*, hang, nut, truth & reconciliation (theatre); second coming (feature film); swirl (short film), random (film); Assata Shakur – The FBI's Most Wanted Woman, lament, gone, random (radio).**

Awards include: **Radio Academy Arias Gold Award (lament); International Film Festival Rotterdam Big Screen Award (second coming); BAFTA for Best Single Drama (random); Black International Film Award for Best UK Film (random); OBIE Special Citation Award (born bad, New York Soho Rep. production); Olivier Award for Most Promising Newcomer (born bad).**

Jamal Ajala (Cast)

Theatre includes: **WW1 (NYT); Something Else (Deafinitely); Stepping Stones (Graeae); Sirens (WeAreZoo).**

Tosin Cole (Cast)

Theatre includes: **They Drink in the Congo (Almeida); Stop (Trafalgar Studios); Sixteen (Gate).**

Television includes: **Doctor Who, Versailles, Lewis, The Secrets, The Cut, E20, Hollyoaks.**

Film includes: **The Souvenir, Burning Sands, Star Wars: The Force Awakens, Unlocked, Gone Too Far, Second Coming, Jasmine.**

Paule Constable (Lighting Designer)

For the Royal Court: **How to Hold Your Breath, Clybourne Park, Posh, The City, Krapps Last Tape, Forty Winks, Boy Gets Girl, Night Songs, The Country, Dublin Carol, The Weir (& West End/Broadway).**

Other theatre includes: **Pericles, Nine Night, Pinocchio, Follies, Angels in America (& Broadway), Mosquitos, Common, Red Barn, Behind the Beautiful Forevers, The Light Princess, Table, This House, The Curious Incident of the Dog in the Night-Time, Phedre, Death & the King's Horseman, War Horse (& West End/Broadway/US tour), Saint Joan, Waves, His Dark Materials (National); The Moderate Soprano (West End); Wolf Hall (& West End/Broadway), The Prince of Homburg, The Seagull, Tales from Ovid, The Dispute, Uncle Vanya, The Mysteries (RSC); Luise Miller, Ivanov (& West End), The Chalk Garden, Othello (Donmar); Happy Days, Feast, The Good Soul of Szechaun, Generations, Vernon God Little (Young Vic); Blasted, Three Sisters (Lyric, Hammersmith); Don Carlos (Crucible, Sheffield /West End); A Midsummer Night's Dream, Peter & Alice, The Cripple of Inishmaan, Privates on Parade (Michael Grandage Co.); Moon for the Misbegotten, Dancing at Lughnasa (Old Vic).**

Dance includes: **The Goldberg Variations (Kim Brandstrup); Seven Deadly Sins (Royal Ballet); Naked (Ballet Boyz); Sleeping Beauty, Dorian Gray, Play Without Words (Matthew Bourne).**

Opera includes: **Carmen, Faust, Rigoletto, The Marriage of Figaro, The Magic Flute, Macbeth (ROH); The Marriage of Figaro, The Cunning Little Vixen, Die Meistersinger, Billy Budd, Rusalka, St Matthew Passion, Cosi Fan Tutte, Giulio Cesare, Carmen, The Double Bill, La Boheme (Glyndebourne); Cosi fan Tutte, Bienvenuto Cellini, Medea, Idomeneo, Satyagraha, Clemenza Di Tito, Gotterdamerung, The Rape of Lucretia, Manon (ENO); Peter Grimes (Opera North); The Marriage of Figaro, The Merry Widow, Don Giovanni, Anna Bolena (The Metropolitan, NYC); Tales of Hoffman (Salzburg Festival); Poppea (Theatre Champs Elysees); Agrippina, A Midsummer Night's Dream, Cosi, The Ring Cycle (Opera National du Rhin); Tristan und Isolde (New National Opera, Tokyo).**

Paule has been the recipient of 4 Olivier Awards, a Tony Award and both the LA and New York Critics Circle Awards. She is an associate at the National Theatre.

Seroca Davis (Cast)

For the Royal Court: **random, 93.2fm.**

Other theatre includes: **Love's Labour's Lost (& US tour), We the People (Globe); Don Juan in Soho (Donmar); Master Juba Project (Albany); Little Sweet Thing (UK tour); Little Baby Jesus (Ovalhouse); With a Little Bit of Luck (Roundhouse).**

Television includes: **Doctor Who, Holby City, Criminal Justice, That Mitchell & Webb Look, Horne & Corden, The Bill, Prime Suspect 7, More Than Love, Comin' Atcha!, Homework High, Daylight Robbery II, Snap, Understanding Electricity.**

Film includes: **second coming.**

Awards include: **Manchester Evening News Award for Best Actress (Little Sweet Thing).**

George Eggay (Cast)

Theatre includes: **King Lear (Old Vic); The Tiger's Bones (New Perspectives); Arabian Nights (New Vic, Stoke on Trent); Dishoodbe On TV (Hackney Empire); Passage to Freedom, This Accursed Thing (Andrew Ashmore Associates); A Streetcar Named Desire, Frozen, The Power Book, The Wind in the Willows (National); Papa Mas (Told By An Idiot); The Ramayana (Birmingham Rep/National); Starstruck (Tricycle); Servant of Two Masters (Nottingham Playhouse); Crossfire (Paines Plough); Bretevski Street (Theatre Centre); The Robbers (Gate); The Love of the Nightingale (Theatre Mélange); The Meeting (Riverside Studios).**

Television includes: **The Forgiving Earth, The Love of Books, Doctors, Shoot the Messenger, Spooks, Between the Lines.**

Film includes: **All You Need is Kill, Final Passage.**

Radio includes: **A Noise in the Night.**

Demetri Goritsas (Cast)

For the Royal Court: **The Sweetest Swing in Baseball, Boy Gets Girl.**

Other theatre includes: **Machinal, Mr Burns (Almeida); All the President's Men?, His Girl Friday, A Prayer for Owen Meaney, Finding the Sun (National); Last of the Boys (Southwark); Amadeus (Theatre North West); Assassins (Library); Street Scene (ENO).**

Television includes: **Ransom, Modus, Black Mirror, Angel of Decay, A Poet in New York, Nixon's the One, Episodes, Twenty Twelve, Souvenir, The Special Relationship, Clouds Over the Hill, Torchwood, Spooks, The Path to 9–11, Numb3rs, Cracker, Gallipoli, Search, Baddiel's Syndrome, The New Addams Family, Viper, Millennium, The Sentinel, Smudge, The Prisoner of Zenda Inc.,** The Annette Funicello Story, Highlander.

Film includes: **Radioactive, The Catcher Was a Spy, Papillon, Darkest Hour, Borg McEnroe, Wichita, Snowden, Everest, Rush, Good Vibrations, Austenland, X-Men: First Class, Acts of Godfrey, The Whistleblower, Genova, A Mighty Heart, Road to Guantanamo, Thunderbirds, Sky Captain & the World of Tomorrow, That Deadwood Feeling, Spy Game, The Bourne Identity, Saving Private Ryan, Excess Baggage, Little Women.**

Radio includes: **Life on Egg, Lou Reed: A Life, Poetry Please, The Cemetery Confessions, Peyton Place.**

Michelle Greenidge (Cast)

Theatre includes: **Nine Night (National); People Who Need People (Vault Festival); The House They Grew Up In (Chichester); Stopcock, Do You Pray? (Southwark/Theatre503); House (Edinburgh Festival/Yard); All Saints (King's Head); At the Feet of Jesus, Super Skinny Bitches (Theatre Royal, Stratford East); Omega Time (White Bear).**

Television includes: **Timewasters, After Life, Code 404, Casualty, Doctors, Invaders, Venus Vs Mars, All About the McKenzies.**

Film includes: **The Come Up, The Intent, Free, Perceptions.**

Merle Hensel (Designer)

For the Royal Court: **a profoundly affectionate, passionate devotion to someone (-noun), X, The Mistress Contract.**

Other theatre includes: **Enemy of the People (Guthrie Theater, Minneapolis); Macbeth [costume] (Young Vic); Arden of Faversham (RSC); Much Ado About Nothing (Royal Exchange, Manchester); Protest Song (National); Macbeth (National Theatre of Scotland/Lincoln Center, NYC/Broadway/Japan tour); Green Snake (National Theatre of China); Glasgow Girls (& National tour), 27, The Wheel (National Theatre of Scotland); The Shawl, Parallel Elektra (Young Vic); Shun-Kin (Complicite); The Girls of Slender Means (Stellar Quines Theatre Company); Diener Zweier Herren (Schloss-theater, Vienna); Ippolit (& Schauspielhaus, Zürich/Münchner Kammerspiele), Der Verlorene (Sophiensaele, Berlin); Kupsch (Deutsches Theater, Göttingen).**

Dance includes: **Contagion (Shobana Jeyasingh Dance); 8 Minutes (Alexander Whitley Dance Company); Tenebre (Ballett am Rhein); The Barbarians in Love [costume], Sun, Political Mother (Hofesh Schechter Company); Lovesong (Frantic Assembly); James Son of James, The Bull, The Flowerbed (Fabulous Beast Dance Theatre); Justitia, Park (Jasmin Vardimon Dance Company); Human Shadows (Underground7/Place Prize).**

Opera includes: **Maria Stuarda (Vereinigte Bühnen, Mönchengladbach/Krefeld); Der Vetter Aus Dingsda (Oper Graz); Lunatics (Kunstfest Weimar); Münchhausen – Herr Der Lügen (Neuköllner Oper, Berlin).**

Film includes: **Morituri Te Salutant, Baby.**

Merle works internationally in a wide variety of styles and genres. She is also a lecturer at Central St Martins School of Art & Design in London. Other teaching includes Rose Bruford College and Goldsmiths.

Eric Kofi Abrefa (Cast)

For the Royal Court: **Choir Boy.**

Other theatre includes: **Julie, A Taste of Honey, The Amen Corner (National); One Love: The Bob Marley Musical (Birmingham Rep); Wildefire, Labyrinth (Hampstead); The Glass Menagerie (UK tour); The Sluts of Sutton Drive (Finborough); Khadij Is 18 (Hackney Empire); Sexy Buffting (Metal Mouth).**

Television includes: **Harlots, Informer, King Lear, Deep State, Jack Ryan, Humans, Lucky Man, HALO: Nightfall, Law & Order, Stella, The Bill, Holby City.**

Film includes: **Jurassic World: Fallen Kingdom, Snowden, I.T, Night of the Lotus, HALO, Fury, Shoot the Messenger, Tight Jeans (short).**

Fiona Lamptey (Film Producer)

Fiona started her career at Channel 4 where she worked on award-winning programmes in documentary, studio and live entertainment. She then went on to work for Film4 where she oversaw low budget and short film production. In 2013 Fiona set up Fruit Tree Media, a boutique production company with a passion to nurture emerging filmmaking talent and cultivate creative partnerships between experienced and inexperienced filmmakers. Fiona's projects have screened at film festivals worldwide, including London Film Festival, SXSW, Palm Springs and Encounters and she was the winner of the Underwire Best Producer Award.

ear for eye marks the third project debbie and Fiona have worked on together; previous projects include *second coming* and *swirl.*

Lashana Lynch (Cast)

For the Royal Court: **a profoundly affectionate, passionate devotion to someone *(-noun).***

Other theatre includes: **Educating Rita (Chichester); Dog Days (Theatre503); Roadkill (Pachamama); Romeo & Juliet (National); 364 (Lyric, Hammersmith); Some Like It Hip Hop (Sadler's Wells); Slave (Lowry); The Frontline,**

The Colour of Justice (Arts Ed).

Television includes: **Y, Bulletproof, Still Star-Crossed, Silent Witness, Death in Paradise, Atlantis, Top Coppers, Crims, The 7.39.**

Film includes: **Captain Marvel, Brotherhood, Powder Room, Fast Girls.**

Vicki Manderson
(Movement Director)

For the Royal Court: **Instructions for Correct Assembly, a profoundly affectionate, passionate devotion to someone *(-noun)*, The Children, The Twits [as associate].**

Other theatre includes: **Square Go (Francesca Moody Productions/Paines Plough); Br'er Cotton (Theatre503); Queen Margaret, Happy Days, The Almighty Sometimes (Royal Exchange, Manchester); Cockpit (Lyceum, Edinburgh); We're Still Here (National Theatre Wales); Jimmy's Hall (Abbey, Dublin); 306 (National Theatre of Scotland); See Me Now (Young Vic); Details (Grid Iron); Housed (Old Vic New Voices).**

Film includes: **swirl.**

As associate movement director, theatre includes: **Let the Right One In (National Theatre of Scotland/ Royal Court/West End/St Ann's, NYC); In Time O' Strife, Black Watch (National Theatre of Scotland); The Curious Incident of the Dog in the Night-Time (National/West End).**

Hayden McLean (Cast)

Theatre includes: **The Cherry Orchard (Royal Exchange, Manchester/Bristol Old Vic); Timbuktu (Ovalhouse); Ages (Old Vic).**

Film includes: **Behind Closed Doors.**

Kayla Meikle (Cast)

For the Royal Court: **Primetime.**

Other theatre includes: **Dance Nation (Almeida); A Midsummer Night's Dream, Jack & the Beanstalk (Lyric, Hammersmith); I Have a Mouth & I Will Scream, People Who Need People, Streets (Vaults Festival); Macbeth, Romeo & Juliet (National); The Taming of the Shrew (Arts); Operation Black Antler (Blast Theory); Merlin (Nuffield); All That Lives (Ovalhouse).**

Television includes: **Afterlife, Will, Bitesize Learning.**

Film includes: **Soundproof, State Zero, Every Eight Minutes, Samira's Party.**

Shaniqua Okwok (Cast)

For the Royal Court: **Instructions for Correct Assembly.**

Television includes: **Shakespeare & Hathaway – Private Investigators.**

Awards include: **Doreen Jones Bursary, The Clive Daley Award.**

Nicholas Pinnock (Cast)

Theatre includes: **The Royale (Bush); Top Dog Underdog (Citizens); Portraits of a Posterity (Arcola); Born Bad (Hampstead); San Diego (Tron); Clear Water (Barbican); Dutchman (Etcetra).**

Television includes: **Counterpart I & II, Guerrilla, Marcella, Midwinter of the Spirit, AD, Fortitude, Mandela: The Prison Years, Ice Cream Girls, Top Boy, The Deep, Diamonds, Coming to England, In Deep, Second Sight: Kingdom of the Blind, Peak Practice, Desmond's.**

Film includes: **Monsters: Dark Continent, The Keeping Room, Captain America, Little Foxes.**

Sarah Quist (Cast)

Theatre includes: **The Captive Queen (Globe); Fox on the Fairway (Hornchurch); Travesties (West End); King Lear (Royal Exchange, Manchester); The Wind in the Willows, The Merry Wives of Windsor, Romeo & Juliet (Grosvenor Park Open Air, Chester); The Playground (Old Red Lion); The Amen Corner (National); Los Sobrinos del Capitán Grant (Teatro de la Zarzuela, Madrid); The Lion King (Disney Land, Paris); The Bacchae (National Theatre of Scotland); A Mad World My Masters, The Tempest, Hecuba, Alice in Wonderland (RSC).**

Television includes: **Stella, Doctors, A Voice from Afar.**

Anita Reynolds (Cast)

Theatre includes: **Absolute Hell (National); hang (The Other Room); The Lion the Witch & the Wardrobe, Arabian Nights, Horrible Histories, Romeo & Juliet, Measure for Measure (Sherman); Speechless (Shared Experience); The Move (Made in Wales); Carers (Turning Point); Cinderella (Unicorn); Forbidden Fruit (Nottingham Playhouse); Wishful Thinking (Hijinx); Dealing with Feelings (London Bubble); How High is Up, Mirror Mirror (Theatre Centre).**

Television includes: **Relik, Keeping Faith, Casualty, Stella, Holby City, Gwaith Cartef, Talking to the Dead, Being Human, Caerdydd, Belonging, Dau Dy A Ni, Nice Day for a Welsh Wedding, The Story of Tracy Beaker, Bay College, Nuts & Bolts, Pobol Y Cwm, The Bench, The Hull Project.**

Radio includes: **Station Road.**

Deepa Shastri (Deaf Consultant)

As BSL consultant, theatre includes: **The Meeting (Chichester); Not I (BAC).**

Dance includes: **Snow (Holly Noble Dance); Puzzle Creature (Neon Dance); Moon (2Faced Dance Company); Candoco (The Space).**
Television includes: **Grantchester.**

As performer, theatre includes: **Frozen (Birmingham Rep).**

As performer, television & film includes: **Deaf Funny, Hands Solo, The Kiss, Rush, Switch, Hear No Evil.**

Deepa has twelve years' experience working in the cultural sector as a Deaf theatre access consultant, BSL performer, BSL consultant and translator. She was a storyteller for BBC Online helping to improve Deaf children's literacy skills and performed a sign song on the main stage as part of the London 2012 Paralympics Opening Ceremony.

Christopher Shutt
(Sound Designer)

For the Royal Court: **a profoundly affectionate, passionate devotion to someone** *(-noun)*, **Escaped Alone, The Sewing Group, hang, Love & Information (& Minetta Lane, NYC), Kin, Aunt Dan & Lemon, Bliss, Free Outgoing, The Arsonists, Serious Money, Road.**

Other theatre includes: **Antony & Cleopatra, Julie, John, Twelfth Night, Here We Go, The Beaux Stratagem, Man & Superman, The James Plays (I & II), From Morning to Midnight, Strange Interlude, Timon of Athens, The Last of the Haussmans, The White Guard, Burnt by the Sun, Every Good Boy Deserves Favour, The Hour We Knew Nothing of Each Other, War Horse (& West End), Philistines, Happy Days, Thérèse Raquin, The Seagull, Burn/Chatroom/ Citizenship, Coram Boy, A Dream Play, A Minute Too Late, Measure for Measure, Mourning Becomes Elektra, Play Without Words, Machinal (National); Aristocrats, Saint Joan, Faith Healer, St Nicholas, Privacy, The Same Deep Water As Me, Philadelphia Here I Come!, Piaf, The Man Who Had All the Luck, Hecuba (Donmar); Nightfall (Bridge); Wild (Hampstead); The Merchant of Venice (Globe); The Entertainer, The Winter's Tale (West End); The Father (Theatre Royal, Bath/Tricycle/West End); Hamlet (Barbican); Bull (Young Vic); The Playboy of the Western World, All About My Mother, Life x 3 (Old Vic); Ruined, Judgement Day (Almeida); Desire Under the Elms, Blasted (Lyric, Hammersmith); A Human Being Died That Night, And No More Shall We Part, For Once (Hampstead); Thyestes (Arcola); Shoes (Sadler's Wells); The Caretaker (Crucible, Sheffield/Tricycle); Julius Caesar (Barbican); Oppenheimer (& West End), Macbeth, The Two Gentlemen of Verona, Wendy & Peter Pan, Candide, Twelfth Night, The Comedy of Errors, The Tempest, King Lear, Romeo & Juliet,**

Noughts & Crosses, King John, Much Ado About Nothing (RSC); Macbeth (Manchester International Festival/New York); Drum Belly (Abbey); Crave/4:48 Psychosis (Sheffield Theatres); Far Away, A Midsummer Night's Dream (Bristol Old Vic); Good (Royal Exchange, Manchester); Man of Aran (Druid, Galway); Country Girls, The House of Special Purpose (Chichester); Little Otik, The Bacchae (National Theatre of Scotland); Riders to the Sea (ENO); A Disappearing Number, The Elephant Vanishes, Mnemonic, The Noise of Time, The Street of Crocodiles, The Three Lives of Lucie Cabrol, The Caucasian Chalk Circle (Complicite); A Human Being Died That Night, Macbeth, All My Sons, The Resistible Rise of Arturo Ui, Happy Days, A Moon for the Misbegotten, Coram Boy, Humble Boy, Not About Nightingales, Mnemonic (Broadway).

Awards include: **Tony Award for Best Sound Design of a Play (War Horse); New York Drama Desk Award for Outstanding Sound Design (Mnemonic, Not About Nightingales).**

Anthony Simpson-Pike
(Assistant Director)

For the Royal Court: **Father Comes Home from the Wars (Parts 1, 2 & 3), Welcome to England [as director](Young Court).**

As director, other theatre includes: **Harambee (Gate); Loyalty & Dissent (& National Archives), Over to You (Tamasha/Rich Mix); Dreamless Sleep (Bunker); Detox (Artistic Directors of the Future); Pandora (Peckham Pelican/Zedel/New River Studios); Coma (Southwark); Something to Say (St James); Plunder (Fresh Direction, Young Vic); Camp (Etcetera/Bussey Building); One for the Road, New World Order (site specific).**

As assistant director, other theatre includes: **Parallel Macbeth (Young Vic); Much Ado About Nothing (Globe).**

Anthony is associate director at the Gate.

Faz Singhateh (Cast)

Theatre includes: **Jesus Hopped the A Train (Home, Manchester); King Lear (Globe); Othello, Someone to Watch Over Me (Harrogate); The Lion the Witch & the Wardrobe (Ilkley Playhouse); Macbeth (Feel Good); Much Ado About Nothing (Liverpool Playhouse); Macbeth (Northcott); Romeo & Juliet, On My Birthday (Royal Exchange, Manchester); The Duchess of Malfi (Salisbury Playhouse); A Raisin in the Sun (Young Vic); Henry V (National); Twelfth Night (Birmingham Rep).**

Television includes: **Coronation Street, Emmerdale, Waterloo Road, Casualty.**

Angela Wynter (Cast)

Theatre includes: **Zebra Crossing II (Talawa); Simply Heavenly (Young Vic); A Christmas Carol (Birmingham Rep); Meetings (Hampstead); Zumbi (BlackTheatre co-op); Jack & the Beanstalk (Lyric, Hammersmith); Boi Boi is Dead (West Yorkshire Playhouse); Raisin in the Sun (Crucible, Sheffield); Lion King (West End).**

Television includes: **Doctors, Holby City, EastEnders, No Problem, Now What, Les Misérables, Clean Break, The Tunnel, Death in Paradise, Vera.**

Film includes: **Wondrous Oblivion, Elphida, Burning an Illusion.**

Radio includes: **The Fisherman, The House of Mr Biswas, Minty Alley, Hurricane Dub, Miguel Street, Rudys Rare Records.**

Angela is a member of the Reggae band Abba Kush.

THE ROYAL COURT THEATRE

The Royal Court Theatre is the writers' theatre. It is a leading force in world theatre for energetically cultivating writers – undiscovered, emerging and established.

Through the writers, the Royal Court is at the forefront of creating restless, alert, provocative theatre about now. We open our doors to the unheard voices and free thinkers that, through their writing, change our way of seeing.

Over 120,000 people visit the Royal Court in Sloane Square, London, each year and many thousands more see our work elsewhere through transfers to the West End and New York, UK and international tours, digital platforms, our residencies across London, and our site-specific work. Through all our work we strive to inspire audiences and influence future writers with radical thinking and provocative discussion.

The Royal Court's extensive development activity encompasses a diverse range of writers and artists and includes an ongoing programme of writers' attachments, readings, workshops and playwriting groups. Twenty years of the International Department's pioneering work around the world means the Royal Court has relationships with writers on every continent.

Within the past sixty years, John Osborne, Samuel Beckett, Arnold Wesker, Ann Jellicoe, Howard Brenton and David Hare have started their careers at the Court. Many others including Caryl Churchill, Athol Fugard, Mark Ravenhill, Simon Stephens, debbie tucker green, Sarah Kane – and, more recently, Lucy Kirkwood, Nick Payne, Penelope Skinner and Alistair McDowall – have followed.

The Royal Court has produced many iconic plays from Lucy Kirkwood's **The Children** to Jez Butterworth's **Jerusalem** and Martin McDonagh's **Hangmen**.

Royal Court plays from every decade are now performed on stage and taught in classrooms and universities across the globe.

It is because of this commitment to the writer that we believe there is no more important theatre in the world than the Royal Court.

Supported using public funding by
ARTS COUNCIL ENGLAND

ROYAL

COMING UP AT THE ROYAL COURT

31 Oct - 17 Nov
Still No Idea
**Lisa Hammond and
Rachael Spence**
with Improbable and the Royal Court Theatre.

28 Nov - 12 Jan
Hole
By Ellie Kendrick
Hole is part of the Royal Court's Jerwood New Playwrights
programme, supported by Jerwood Charitable Foundation.

6 Dec - 26 Jan
The Cane
By Mark Ravenhill

14 Feb – 16 Mar
Cyprus Avenue
By David Ireland
A Royal Court and Abbey Theatre Production.

Become a Friend of the Royal Court for just £35 a year and
take advantage of exclusive benefits including priority booking and advance
access to our £12 Monday tickets in the Jerwood Theatre Downstairs. For
more information visit **royalcourttheatre.com/support-us**

Tickets from £12
royalcourttheatre.com

Sloane Square London, SW1W 8AS ⊖ Sloane Square
⇌ Victoria Station 🐦 royalcourt 📘 royalcourttheatre

 ARTS COUNCIL ENGLAND JERWOOD CHARITABLE FOUNDATION

ROYAL

ASSISTED PERFORMANCES

Captioned Performances

Captioned performances are accessible for deaf, deafened & hard of hearing people as well as being suitable for people for whom English is not a first language.

Still No Idea: Thu 8 Nov 2018, 7.45pm (speech-to-text post-show talk); Wed 14 Nov, 7.45pm.
ear for eye: Thu 8 Nov, 2.30pm; Thu 15 Nov, 7.30pm; Thu 22 Nov, 2.30pm & 7.30pm.
Hole: Wed 2 Jan 2019, 7.45pm.
The Cane: Tue 8 Jan 2019, 7.30pm; Fri 18 Jan 2019, 7.30pm.

Audio Described Performances

Audio described performances are accessible for blind or partially sighted patrons. They are preceded by a touch tour which offers access to elements of theatre design including set & costume.

Still No Idea: Sat 10 Nov 2018, 7.45pm (touch tour 6.15pm).
ear for eye: Sat 17 Nov 2018, 2.30pm (touch tour at 1pm).
The Cane: Sat 19 Jan 2019, 2.30pm (touch tour at 1pm).

COURT

ROYAL

ASSISTED PERFORMANCES

BSL Interpreted Performances

BSL (British Sign Language) interpreted performances give D/deaf BSL users access to the spoken content of the performance.

Still No Idea: Fri 16 Nov 2018, 7.45pm.
ear for eye: Sat 24 Nov, 7.30pm.

Relaxed Environment Performances

All relaxed environment performances are suitable for those who would benefit from a more relaxed atmosphere inside the auditoria. House lights may remain raised slightly, patrons can enter and exit the auditorium as needed and there is a relaxed attitude to noise in the auditorium. For some productions small changes may be made to the performances including the lighting/sound but no changes will be made to the text.

Still No Idea: All performances 31 Oct – 17 Nov 2018.
The Cane: Mon 14 Jan 2019, 7.30pm.

For more information and to book access tickets online, visit

royalcourttheatre.com/assisted-performances

Sloane Square London, SW1W 8AS ⊖ Sloane Square ⇌ Victoria Station
🐦 royalcourt 📘 royalcourttheatre

COURT

ROYAL COURT SUPPORTERS

The Royal Court is a registered charity and not-for-profit company. We need to raise £1.5 million every year in addition to our core grant from the Arts Council and our ticket income to achieve what we do.

We have significant and longstanding relationships with many generous organisations and individuals who provide vital support. Royal Court supporters enable us to remain the writers' theatre, find stories from everywhere and create theatre for everyone.

We can't do it without you.

PUBLIC FUNDING

Arts Council England, London
British Council

TRUSTS & FOUNDATIONS

The Backstage Trust
The Bryan Adams Charitable Trust
The Austin & Hope Pilkington Trust
The Boshier-Hinton Foundation
Martin Bowley Charitable Trust
The Chapman Charitable Trust
Gerald Chapman Fund
CHK Charities
The City Bridge Trust
The Clifford Chance Foundation
Cockayne - Grants for the Arts
The Ernest Cook Trust
The Nöel Coward Foundation
Cowley Charitable Trust
The Eranda Rothschild Foundation
Lady Antonia Fraser for The Pinter Commission
Genesis Foundation
The Golden Bottle Trust
The Haberdashers' Company
The Paul Hamlyn Foundation
Roderick & Elizabeth Jack
Jerwood Charitable Foundation
The Leche Trust
The Andrew Lloyd Webber Foundation

The London Community Foundation
John Lyon's Charity
The Mackintosh Foundation
Clare McIntyre's Bursary
Old Possum's Practical Trust
The Andrew W. Mellon Foundation
The David & Elaine Potter Foundation
The Richard Radcliffe Charitable Trust
Rose Foundation
Royal Victoria Hall Foundation
The Sackler Trust
The Sobell Foundation
Span Trust
John Thaw Foundation
Unity Theatre Trust
The Wellcome Trust
The Garfield Weston Foundation

CORPORATE SPONSORS

Aqua Financial Solutions Ltd
Cadogan Estates
Colbert
Edwardian Hotels, London
Fever-Tree
Gedye & Sons
Greene King
Kirkland & Ellis International LLP
Kudos
MAC
Room One
Sister Pictures
Sky Drama

CORPORATE MEMBERS

Gold
Weil, Gotshal & Manges LLP

Silver
Auerbach & Steele Opticians
Bloomberg
Cream
Kekst CNC
Left Bank Pictures
PATRIZIA
Tetragon Financial Group

For more information or to become a foundation or business supporter contact Camilla Start: camillastart@royalcourttheatre.com/020 7565 5064.

ROYAL

BAR & KITCHEN

The Royal Court's Bar & Kitchen aims to create a welcoming and inspiring environment with a style and ethos that reflects the work we put on stage. Our menu, created by Head Chef David Adams, consists of simple, ingredient driven and flavour-focused dishes with an emphasis on freshness and seasonality. This is supported by a carefully curated drinks list notable for its excellent wine selection, craft beers and skilfully prepared coffee. By day a perfect spot for long lunches, meetings or quiet reflection and by night an atmospheric, vibrant meeting space for cast, crew, audiences and the general public.

GENERAL OPENING HOURS
Monday – Friday: 10am – late
Saturday: 12noon – late

Advance booking is suggested at peak times.

For more information and to book access tickets online, visit

royalcourttheatre.com/bar

HIRES & EVENTS

The Royal Court is available to hire for celebrations, rehearsals, meetings, filming, ceremonies and much more. Our two theatre spaces can be hired for conferences and showcases, and the building is a unique venue for bespoke weddings and receptions.

For more information and to book access tickets online, visit

royalcourttheatre.com/events

Sloane Square London, SW1W 8AS Sloane Square Victoria Station
 royalcourt royalcourttheatre

COURT

"There are no spaces, no rooms in my opinion, with a greater legacy of fearlessness, truth and clarity than this space."
Simon Stephens, Associate Playwright

The Royal Court invests in the future of the theatre, offering writers the support, time and resources to find their voices and tell their stories, asking the big questions and responding to the issues of the moment.

As a registered charity, the Royal Court needs to raise at least £1.5 million every year in addition to our Arts Council funding and ticket income, to keep seeking out, developing and nurturing new voices. Please join us by donating today.

You can donate online at **royalcourttheatre.com/donate** or via our **donation box in the Bar & Kitchen.**

We can't do it without you.

Writing the Future

To find out more about the different ways in which you can be involved please contact Charlotte Cole on 020 7565 5049 / charlottecole@royalcourttheatre.com

The English Stage Company at the Royal Court Theatre is a registered charity (No. 231242).

ear for eye

parts one, two and three

debbie tucker green

2

Characters

PART ONE

Scene One, US, African Americans
SON, *teenager*
MOM

Scene Two, US, African Americans
OLDER MAN *or* OLDER WOMAN
YOUNG WOMAN, *student, approximate age nineteen, same character as in Scene Ten*

Scene Three, UK, Black British
WOMAN

Scenes Four, Seven, Nine, Twelve, US, African Americans
ADULT, *male*
YOUNG ADULT, *male*

Scene Five, UK, Black British
FRIEND 1, *female*
FRIEND 2, *female*

Scene Six, US, African Americans
SON, *same character as in Scene One*
MOM, *same character as in Scene One*
DAD

Scene Eight, UK, Black British
MUM
DAD
SON, *teenager*

Scene Ten, US, African American
YOUNG WOMAN, *same character as in Scene Two*

Scene Eleven, UK, Black British
MAN

PART TWO – US

FEMALE, *African American, twenties*
MALE, *Caucasian American, fifties*

PART THREE

Scene One, US, pre-filmed
Various Caucasian non-actors/actors. Approximately thirty speaking parts

Scene Two, UK, pre-filmed
Various Caucasian non-actors/actors. Approximately twenty-five speaking parts

EPILOGUE (onstage)

ADULT (US), *same character from Part One*
YOUNG ADULT (US), *same character from Part One*
YOUNG WOMAN (US), *same character from Part One*
MAN (UK), *same character from Part One*

Part One contains fifteen characters; Part Two has two characters; Part Three has fifty-five speaking parts (filmed).

No direct address to audience.

A forward slash (/) in dialogue is an overlapping point.

Words in brackets ( ) are intention only and not to be spoken.

This text went to press before the end of rehearsals and so may differ slightly from the play as performed.

PART ONE

Scene One

US.
African Americans.

SON	So if I put my hands up –
MOM	a threat, threatening.
SON	Slowly?
MOM	Provocative.
SON	Showed my palms
MOM	inflammatory. Could be.
SON	…(If I) raised my hands just to –
MOM	no
SON	to just –
MOM	no
SON	but
MOM	aggression
SON	but just to show that they're –
MOM	an act of / aggression
SON	that I'm –
MOM	that won't work, that doesn't work Son.
	SON *thinks*.
SON	If I left them down?
MOM	Belligerent.
SON	By my side – ?
MOM	Attitude.

SON	(Hands) in pockets?
MOM	Concealing.
SON	Jacket pockets –
MOM	obscuring
SON	pants pockets –
MOM	cocky
SON	hands together – ?
MOM	Masking
SON	what but / what?
MOM	I know / Son.
SON	My hands together – ?
MOM	Sarcastic –
SON	but
MOM	challenging
SON	but –
MOM	provocative. Which is… can be, is… Incendiary. To them.
SON	…Holding hands-holding hands – *c'mon* –
MOM	collusion complicity
SON	behind my back –
MOM	attitude – arrogance insolence ignorance defiance
SON	gesturing that I –
MOM	aggressive
SON	that I –
MOM	aggressive

SON	that I
MOM	aggressive
SON	but I –
MOM	I know
SON	but that I –
MOM	I know Son.
SON	…So gesturing…?
MOM	Antagonistic.
SON	
SON	Shrugging?
MOM	Ignorant.
SON	Just –
MOM	just
SON	just?
MOM	…Just. Hostile.
SON	But –
MOM	hostile
SON	but – ?
MOM	But. Son.
	SON *thinks hard.*
SON	…Right.
MOM	Not right.
SON	Right.
	Beat. MOM *shakes her head a little.*
	If I look…
	She watches him.

	If I look at them –
MOM	bold
SON	confidently look at / them.
MOM	confrontational
SON	as a –
MOM	audacious
SON	as a man – which you said was good
MOM	it is good
SON	as a man / then –
MOM	forward, forthright –
SON	which you said was good
MOM	it is good Son
SON	'confident' which you said –
MOM	I did – do
SON	said was –
MOM	I did
SON	how you raised me –
MOM	I did
SON	so, confident…
MOM	
SON	Confidence.
MOM	
SON	Confidently…
MOM	
SON	Mom?
MOM	
SON	Right.
MOM	…It's good but not good.

SON	But –
MOM	it is but it's not.
SON	But – .
MOM SON	
SON	If I look away –
MOM	evasive elusive ambiguous
SON	but if / I –
MOM	cagey and –
SON	but what if I-I – but – ?
SON	
SON	If I turn away – .

MOM *shakes her head*.

If I turn – Mom, turn away to –

MOM	that –
SON	*Mom*, turn away to go to make like – if I –
MOM	no
SON	turn away to walk away
MOM	Son – .
SON	Turn so that I –
MOM	no
SON	so then I –
MOM	no
SON	but I would be –
MOM	no
SON	Mom
MOM	impudence

SON	Mom?
MOM	Disobedience
SON	Mom
MOM	impertinence
SON	but I'd be –
MOM	no. Don't turn your back, don't turn your back.
MOM	

Beat.

SON	…Mom.

Beat.

If I look away to avoid looking at –

MOM	guilty
SON	but-but if I look like I'm looking but just look past y'know –
MOM	no
SON	if I look like / that – ?
MOM	no no no. Doesn't work, that –
SON	if I –
MOM	doesn't work
SON	but if I –
MOM	won't work
SON	if I look at the floor –
MOM	*hell no*, we didn't raise you to look at no floor Son.
SON	If I – but if I… Then… But-but if I – .

He thinks.

Then-then…

Scene Two

US.
African Americans.

OLDER (WO)MAN   Before the sun got cold (and) turn't the
skies to grey…
Before the wind got busy and rain decided
it couldn't be fucked to fall.
Before the seasons decided they weren't
worth changing
we wasn't worth the effort
we weren't worth changing for.
Before the green grass browned
before the concrete could warm
before the street lights repeat their on-off
on-off.

Before the cars start up
before the streets start to fill
before the schools open
before the workers work,
before the cleaners clean everybody else's
dirt,
before the night-shifts sleep – before the
day-workers start
before the air gets thick before the air gets
stale, before the air isn't
and-but…
But.

Before the publicity
before the coverage
before the courage
before the placards
before hailers start hailing
before the organised call – the call and
response,
before the slogans
the selfies
the official route, the phone footage,

the T-shirts, the graffiti, the street art,
before the famous, the hi-vis, the groups,
the churches, the congregations, before
makin it family-friendly, sound-bite
friendly, before makin it look, friendly.
Makin us look friendly.

Before – .
Before
leaders appointed themselves
before
speakers lined up to speak,
before people stood up and spoke
stood up and spoke
stood up and spoke for me without askin
me if I needed to be stood and spoke up
for.

Before the hustling positioning
and the hustle for position.
Before those that want to be at the front
to be seen at the front
push up front
bein up front
pushing past
to be present.
To be seen to be seen.
Before – .
Before...

Before the lecterns, before the lectures
before the dirty pigs realised, before the dirty
media realised, before photographers shot,
before it was trending, before it went viral,
before it was 'cool', before names were put
to it, before scholars spoke on it, before
montages were made of it. Before it was
uploaded, downloaded, offloaded, done,
before they tried to dissect it disrespected it
tried to disrupt it, tried to counter it tried to
destroy it before liberals tried to claim it
reinterpret it, appropriate it, before

corporates endorsed it designers got graphic
on it before people made symbols of it,
before they thought they got away with it...

Before all that...

(*Points to him/herself.*)
(We were here.)

Before the dogs spat
and the pigs barked
and the people spat
and the dogs barked
before hateful eyes
more hate-filled
than mouths – and mouths which were
overflowing with their...
When actions
were actively
violent
violently violating us
and inaction was
violent
violently violating us
hate-filled,
hate fuelled. Driven.
Before our children had
no chance
had no chance
to be children,
had no choice
have no choice
but to be
involved.
When involved
was physical
was difficult
was dangerous
is physical
is difficult
is dangerous.
Is relentless.

When marching had consequences
when protest was a risk
when lynching was sport
when living
wasn't,
when they norms
that weren't normal
aren't normal
were called out
are called out
called on
and
challenged.
When ease
wasn't.
When expectation
wasn't.
Before
what's been
idolised
was livin ugly, livin unsure. Insecure.
When what's been sanitised
was messy
was painful
and
what's been epitomised
was
fucking

hard.

Before our losses were reduced
to known names only
reduced to a
fashion.
When in fashion.
Or
forgotten.
Conveniently.
Then denied. Conveniently.

Before our
living

history and herstory
got
gets
is
sanitised, sterilised,
shiny-fied
simplified
by those
who were never there.
Repeatin and repeatin and repeating and
repeatin
a version of us
an abbreviation
a simplification
a narrowing
a lie
that us then repeats as well.

Before those thass sleepin shout loudest
'bout they woke – and how.
The wokest of the wokest of wokedom
confusin those that don't know no better,
confusin theyselves.

Before the dead – our dead turn in they
graves
till they can't turn no more
tossing
in their
unease.

Before-before – . When – .
…Before – .
Before all that… before alla that…

YOUNG WOMAN

OLDER (WO)MAN   I was here.

I was here – I was we was we (was) – I
was, here.

YOUNG WOMAN

OLDER (WO)MAN   Is all I'm sayin.

YOUNG WOMAN   …It's not a competition.

OLDER (WO)MAN   It's not no competition.

YOUNG WOMAN   It's not a –

OLDER (WO)MAN   but
if it was… we woulda won.
Only shit we woulda won.

Fuck, it's cold.

Scene Three

UK.
Black British.

She shivers. She is talking to someone.

WOMAN   Y'know...
                         When I was sitting in that cell
                         they sat down by me and told me
                         what they could say to you.

                         When I was picked up and di'unt know
                         why
                         and asked.
                         And asked.

                         When they told me I was
                         'bein aggressive'
                         when I weren't.

                         When they said I was shouting
                         when I was speaking
                         then changed it to I was
                         'acting aggressive'
                         when I weren't. I was just askin.
                         When they wouldn't answer me when I
                         asked them what 'acting aggressive' was.
                         When they changed it to,
                         I was
                         'talkin aggressive' which I weren't
                         when they joked, to themselves – not to me
                         – that we all sound aggressive to them
                         anyway.

                         When they said I was bein
                         'provocative'
                         and I asked them
                         'how'
                         and they said
                         'physically'
                         and I asked them
                         'how – ?' when there's four-more-of-them

than the one-a-me and they said askin was
provocative and I said asking ain't physical
and they said 'your mouth will get you into
trouble so best you shut up'.

When I asked them
'why me' and they smiled
'fits the description of'
and the third-of-the-four-of-them smiled
wider knowin that I didn't and knowing
that I knew I didn't and the description
they described was so shit it was laughable.
If it was laughable.
When they said – the second-of-the-four –
that I was gesturing aggressively and my
hands said a passive 'how' and the third-a-
the-four-a-them cuffed them saying
'See'.
When they told me to stop speakin
so I stopped speakin… but then I started
shoutin – I did start shoutin – fuck it and
my people stopped to see and saw seeing
the four-a-them and the one-a-me, and my
people was watching
and witnessing
and waiting
and
some a-the young ones started filming –
phones out like a hi-tech self-defence but
when they were threatened to keep walking
and to stop filming or-or…
It being made clear, clearer than crystal
what would happen to them if they didn't.
So they…

But.

An elder – shouts back:
'Know your rights sister!'
then the third of the four-a-them who had
cuffed me
smiled

and
silent laughed
and
said for my ears only,
that the four-a-them got more rights than
me and they know 'em better than the few I
got that he knew I didn't even know.

I heard myself stop shoutin
I hear myself stop shoutin.
I stopped
cos
cos…

Beat.

And when I stopped
I was silent…

Then they told me my silence could be
used against me in a court of law. When all
I could say is a
'why'
to alla this
they told me I'd
'get all I need to know
down the station'.
When they said my reluctance was
'resistance'
and my hesitation was
'obstruction'
when they dropped
'resisting arrest'
like it was a lyric
droppin me to the concrete like a reflex –
when they said I'm making it worse for
myself – I couldn't think how much more
worse it could be made.
But it could be made…

When I was pushed in the back into the
back of their car.
Cuffs

cuttin my skin
but suckin it up
to not show.
To not show (them).
When they drove me down streets I know
we know
you know
but don't know from the back of their – as
one-of-the-three-of-them in the car – the-
one-in-the-back-with-me tells me to
'Keep still
keep still'
but I can't still myself
even if I wanted to.
I can't be still
sit still.
…Still.

At the lights, them thass curious
look over
look in
look unsurprised, uninterested, indifferent,
look unconcerned
and I look…
(embarrassed.)

When I hold my shaking voice
together
to just about not shake
and steady say
as calmly
as softly
as clearly
as passively
as I can
that,
'I think you have the wrong – '
they say – the-one-in-the-front-not-driving
– turns sharp and says as soft and calm and
clear and… sarcastic as she can that
'Your mouth has already got you here. You
don't learn. Do you.'

And one a them laughed
the one-a-them that was drivin
laughed then caught my eye in the mirror
and pretended he was laughing at
something else.
But wasn't.
So…

When I sat in that cell.

When I sat in that cell.
With the fourth-a-the-four-of-them
standing carefully
quietly
casually
over me
on his ones
tellin me how we, 'become unwell'
can
become 'unwell'
tellin me the…
'suicide rates' of us in their 'care'.

Beat.

Telling me
that they could say to you…

Scene Four

US.
African Americans.

ADULT   …(It) won't make you feel better.

                        Beat.

                        It won't make you feel any / better.

YOUNG ADULT   Gimme a reason to not I / said.

ADULT   It won't make you feel –

YOUNG ADULT   can't make me feel no worse than I feel
                        now.

YOUNG ADULT
ADULT

ADULT   It don't work like that.

YOUNG ADULT

ADULT   You don't –

YOUNG ADULT   you don't / know.

ADULT   you don't work like / that.

YOUNG ADULT   You don't know.

ADULT   I / know you.

YOUNG ADULT   You don't know

ADULT   I know / you.

YOUNG ADULT   Can't be –

ADULT   I. Know. You.

YOUNG ADULT   …Can't be no worse than I feel – than they
                        makin me / feel

ADULT   I know how you / feel.

YOUNG ADULT   than they want to make me feel than they
                        got me feeling –

ADULT   you know I know how you / feel.

YOUNG ADULT   feelin what I feel even when I don't wanna
                 feel it – what?! Even when I fight to not
                 feel it – y'feel me? *You don't know*.

ADULT

YOUNG ADULT   I got other shit to feel. But I got to feelin
                 this. I gots to feel
                 this – .

                 ADULT *nods*.

                 You noddin it –

ADULT   I know

YOUNG ADULT   you don't – you don't know how they
                 fuckin got me wid / this.

ADULT   I wouldn't know and – ?

                 ADULT *is not impressed with the cursing
                 from* YOUNG ADULT. YOUNG ADULT
                 acknowledges his bad language.

YOUNG ADULT   Sorry.

ADULT   I would / know –

YOUNG ADULT   They make me feel…

ADULT

YOUNG ADULT   They make me feel…

ADULT   Alright / now.

YOUNG ADULT   They make me feel –

ADULT   okay / alright.

YOUNG ADULT   and-but this world ain't theirs –

ADULT   c'mon –

YOUNG ADULT   and-and-and I'll take the risk a feeling
                 better –

ADULT   c'mon / now.

YOUNG ADULT   feelin a bit better in a minute –

ADULT	hey, you / done?
YOUNG ADULT	I'll risk feelin better'n *this* cos I reckon I couldn't feel worse'n what I'm feelin now – that they got me feelin now that they got me feelin for (fuckin) years. I got other shit to think about but they denyin me that luxury cos they forcin themselves on me to think about them. I feel *sick*
ADULT	y'need / to –
YOUNG ADULT	not sick-sick but *sick* – they got me feelin some fuckin toxic muthafuckin –
ADULT	lissen –
YOUNG ADULT	scuse my fuckin language
ADULT	alright now. I / know.
YOUNG ADULT	Do you know?
ADULT	I / know.
YOUNG ADULT	Do you feel – ?
ADULT	Course I feel / it.
YOUNG ADULT	You don't –
ADULT	don't insult my –
YOUNG ADULT	then don't insult mine. Wid all due respect.
ADULT	Young'un –
YOUNG ADULT	gimme a reason to –
ADULT	young'un you need to be able / to –
YOUNG ADULT	gimme a reason to / not.
ADULT	y'gonna have to start to –
YOUNG ADULT	to *what*?
	Beat.
ADULT	… You ain't the first.
YOUNG ADULT	

ADULT	Ain't the first, young thing. Nowhere near.
YOUNG ADULT	
YOUNG ADULT	(*Quietly.*) I say I / was?
ADULT	You ain't unique.
YOUNG ADULT	
ADULT	Nu'un boutchu unique.
YOUNG ADULT	
ADULT	You ain't the second or the third even.
YOUNG ADULT	
ADULT	You ain't original
YOUNG ADULT	(I) say I was –
ADULT	nu'un 'bout your shit new. 'Scuse *my* language.'
YOUNG ADULT	I –
ADULT	'no disrespect.'
ADULT YOUNG ADULT	
ADULT	There's been smarter.
YOUNG ADULT	
ADULT	There'll be smarter.
YOUNG ADULT	
ADULT	There is, smarter.
YOUNG ADULT	
ADULT	There's been better. No disrespect.
YOUNG ADULT	
ADULT	There'll be / better – .
YOUNG ADULT	I say I was smartest?
ADULT	

YOUNG ADULT	I say I was the / bestest?
ADULT	There is smarter. There is better.
YOUNG ADULT	
ADULT	Than you.
YOUNG ADULT	
YOUNG ADULT	What – ? You wanna wait on some –
ADULT	so –
YOUNG ADULT	some unique utopia of a somebody – ?
ADULT	So what I / was –
YOUNG ADULT	Some-some-some super-freakin-college-hero of a somebody –
ADULT	mind your / mouth
YOUNG ADULT	some higher-fuckin-bein gon' be on some sorta intervention in this / shit?
ADULT	Mind. Your. / Mouth.
YOUNG ADULT	I don't mean to – and I'm like – y'know – I don't mean to – it juss, but you sit and wait if thass whatchu waitin on / cos –
ADULT	Don't –
YOUNG ADULT	cos I ain't said I was could be was or would be none a / that.
ADULT	don't twist it cos I ain't sayin that iss – y'know I ain't sayin / that it's –
YOUNG ADULT	you waitin on su'un perfect –
ADULT	you don't get to –
YOUNG ADULT	waitin on someone perfect then / you –
ADULT	you don't get to put words in my mouth
YOUNG ADULT	you wait on perfect –
ADULT	you need to / stop
YOUNG ADULT	you wait on perfect – you still waitin

ADULT	you ill-formed, your ill-informed not fully formed half-thinkin words in my mouth – ? (Your) shit words in my mouth? You don't get to do that, I / said –
YOUNG ADULT	Sir I –
ADULT	I said –
YOUNG ADULT	Sir I ain't said, sayin, would say that. 'Bout me. Sir.
ADULT	
YOUNG ADULT	Whatchu said 'bout me. None a that 'bout me I said 'bout myself would say 'bout myself. Ain't said shit 'bout myself like I'm best the best gon' be the best – no. No. So. …Maaan.

Beat.

How you do?
How you do / this?

ADULT	I ain't sayin iss –
YOUNG ADULT	how you even do you? You here you still here you doin you however that be.
ADULT	I do me.
YOUNG ADULT	How? And don't say 'you know'
ADULT	I do me, despite –
YOUNG ADULT	I'm doin me tryin to do me – won't let me be me and ain't 'despitin' nuthin, I'ma change some shit to allow me to be / me.
ADULT	You gon' let me – ?
YOUNG ADULT	Don't wanna 'despite' *nuthin*
ADULT	you gonna let me finish?
YOUNG ADULT	…Didju finish?
ADULT	

YOUNG ADULT	…If you finish whatchu finish we wouldn't be – I wouldn't / be –
ADULT	You gotta short memory and a disrespectful mouth
YOUNG ADULT	I –
ADULT	best you fill one before the other and I suggest you start with what's up here (*Taps head*.) to affect what comes outta there (*Gestures mouth*.) (to) stop you soundin like you stupid.
YOUNG ADULT	
ADULT	
YOUNG ADULT	You march?
ADULT	
YOUNG ADULT	Was you out there?
ADULT	
YOUNG ADULT	You do su'un?
ADULT	
YOUNG ADULT	You change anythin – ?
ADULT	You ain't livin how I've lived so su'un musta –
YOUNG ADULT	this shit ain't livin right.

He wipes some sweat. Hot.

(I'm) fuckin (sweating) – this shit got me sweatin. They make their wrongs sound right. It ain't right. And my shit ain't wrong – how my shit be wrong? What I'm feelin ain't wrong. Right? Ain't wrong in what I'm feelin, wrong is *why* I'm feelin – havinta fuckin feel it. Right? I can *make* my shit sound right if that would make *you* feel better, can make mine sound more right than their wrongs and mine wouldn't

even be wrong, I'd be justified. More'n
justified. Toldju.

ADULT *shakes his head a little.*

Do that all you want.

ADULT   I will.

ADULT *shakes his head a little.*

YOUNG ADULT   Do it again.

ADULT   I / will.

YOUNG ADULT   Don't shake it for me –

ADULT   young'un you tellin me what / to – ?

YOUNG ADULT   No Sir no Sir but – . I said, gimme a reason
                         to not.

YOUNG ADULT
ADULT

ADULT   …It's not easy.

YOUNG ADULT   I ask if it was?

ADULT   Doesn't get any easier –

YOUNG ADULT   I say it did?

ADULT   It's immoral

YOUNG ADULT   gimme a reason, *gimme a reason* c'mon
                         c'mon a good one to / not.

ADULT   it's not an example that should –

YOUNG ADULT   ain't nobody need to follow what I do –
                         I ain't lookin no followers – for followers –
                         I ain't waitin on no nobody to follow me –
                         I say 'follow me'? You hear 'follow me'
                         from me – 'follow me and my morals' after
                         witnessin their immorality? I ain't sayin
                         'follow shit'. People ain't waitin on me,
                         I ain't worth waitin on and I ain't waitin on
                         no / people.

ADULT   It's hard to live with.

YOUNG ADULT	I can live with / it.
ADULT	This sin't in his name –
YOUNG ADULT	he ain't here to specify – thass the *point*.
ADULT	He never said for this
YOUNG ADULT	never said not this and if he still was here maybe he woulda said, 'Do somethin. Do fuckin somethin' maybe he woulda / said –
ADULT	You don't know.
YOUNG ADULT	I woulda said that shit.
ADULT	This isn't you.
YOUNG ADULT	Woulda writ that shit down
ADULT	this sin't about –
YOUNG ADULT	large – capitals
ADULT	not / aboutchu.
YOUNG ADULT	*will* write that shit down on a in-case, leave that shit as my fuckin legacy: '*Do* *somethin*' – (if) that was me, you do somethin? You do somethin – you do something for me?
ADULT	…This isn't about you
YOUNG ADULT	(would) you do something for me if it was – if that / was?
ADULT	it wasn't and / it ain't.
YOUNG ADULT	you do *somethin* for me – *wouldju*?
ADULT YOUNG ADULT	
ADULT	What d'you think.
YOUNG ADULT	
ADULT	What d'you think.

YOUNG ADULT	…And if it ain't in his name there's a fuckin list centuries long of names I could. Would. Will. Do it in. If you ain't gonna give me no good reason to not.
	Beat.
ADULT	…(It) would lead to a bloodbath
YOUNG ADULT	this is a bloodbath.
ADULT	Would lead to a war
YOUNG ADULT	this is a war
ADULT	you couldn't survive the –
YOUNG ADULT	barely surviving now.
ADULT	…It won't help.
YOUNG ADULT	You don't know
ADULT	what you want to help it won't / help.
YOUNG ADULT	you don't know
ADULT	you ain't helpin
YOUNG ADULT	you know?
ADULT	…You ain't helpful.
YOUNG ADULT	
ADULT	Like this.
YOUNG ADULT	Cos, what you doin-not-doing is?
ADULT	
YOUNG ADULT	(*Dry.*) Right?
ADULT YOUNG ADULT	
YOUNG ADULT	Cos…
	How has your shit helped? Is helping? Scuse my (language). Read a book – ? What? Then what? Shake y'head at a article? Then what? See a image, turn over the TV? Walk past

	a protest? *Then what?* Really, how has your shit helped – and I ain't talkin 'bout no dusty shit from way-back-when.
ADULT	
YOUNG ADULT	See.
ADULT	I'm feelin –
YOUNG ADULT	see
ADULT	footprints
YOUNG ADULT	huh?
	ADULT *dusts off his own shoulders.*
ADULT	'Bout size nines. I'm feelin –
YOUNG ADULT	what are / you – ?
ADULT	weight.
YOUNG ADULT	What?
ADULT	Carryin an uncertain, unsteady weight.
YOUNG ADULT ADULT	
ADULT	That ain't mine.
YOUNG ADULT	
ADULT	Whatchu standin on?
YOUNG ADULT	What?
ADULT	Who you standin on?
YOUNG ADULT	Huh?
ADULT	Whose shoulders you standin on young'un? Cos I'm feelin your unfocused, uncertain, unhelpful, unsteady heavy weight on mine – and mine before / mine.
YOUNG ADULT	With respect –
ADULT	(*Dry.*) with all 'due respect' – don't question me – *don't* – you don't got the – you don't have the – go read a book –

thatchu ain't gon' find in no library. Go
lissen to those who lived more'n you, years
over you – gotta a little su'un to say. Lissen
to them that talk quiet not-never-loud and
lissen harder to them that don't say a damn
thing. Find those that say nuthin, and look
how they know – what they know, what
they seen, what they *been*. Look and learn,
lissen and learn (if you) shut your damn
mouth for two minutes you wouldn't have
to be askin half a / your –

YOUNG ADULT   Sir I –

ADULT   and fuck your disrespectful respect.

Beat.

Scuse my fuckin language.

Scene Five

UK.
Black British.

FRIEND 2	Idunsomethin Idunsumthin youseemedosomethin you see-me-do-the-thing-I-dun??!! (I) dun somethin – lissen-lissen – I dun-just-dun – did / something –
FRIEND 1	I / saw.
FRIEND 2	yousee yousee / yousee???
FRIEND 1	I saw I / saw.
FRIEND 2	Was shittin myself (didju) you see?
FRIEND 1	Could / see – .
FRIEND 2	You see-didju see?!
FRIEND 1	I saw could / see.
FRIEND 2	Didju see me – couldja tell I was properly – but / I –
FRIEND 1	You looked / nervous.
FRIEND 2	properly-shittin-myself but – '*nervous*'? – more than that / *truss* mi!
FRIEND 1	Looked properly nervous
FRIEND 2	*shit!* Truss mi whole-heap more'n that –
FRIEND 1	I / know.
FRIEND 2	therein'tevenno – there ain't even no word for what I (felt) – couldn'tseeyou couldn't-see-you couldn't see where you was – I was shittin bricks trust me but I-knew-I-knew-I-knew y'know iss a weird fuckin feeling – a hundred per cent sure tho a hundred per cent over-sure – I think iss that, that a hundred per cent sureness ain't never felt it before ain't never felt nuthin like it ain't never felt that *that* before. *Real*. Iss real – .

	She draws breath – still hyped.
FRIEND 1	Right / right.
FRIEND 2	Aaarrrgh is-like iss like – look at my hands look at my hands they're – can you see my hands?! Look / at –
FRIEND 1	Can see your / hands.
FRIEND 2	look-look-look thass not me doin nuthin thass not me doin anythin thass not me tryin – thassthemontheirown thass not me even looklooklook / – shit.
FRIEND 1	Can see your hands –
FRIEND 2	shit!
FRIEND 1	Adrenalin.
FRIEND 2	Fuckin –
FRIEND 1	adrenalin
	FRIEND 2 *feels her own heart.*
FRIEND 2	feelthatfeelthatfeelthatfeelthat –
FRIEND 1	I know
FRIEND 2	*feel* it
FRIEND 1	I can see –
FRIEND 2	you can't see *feel* it – *fuck* iss thru my fuckin chest pumpin like a fuckin (I) could have a heart attack (I) coulda had a heart attack. I could be havin a / fuckin –
FRIEND 1	You're not havin no heart / attack.
FRIEND 2	fuck-it can you catch a asthma or summink – ? I ain't even asthmatic or nuthin but it feels like it / feels like –
FRIEND 1	You ain't havin no asthma / attack.
FRIEND 2	feelslikeitfeelslike –
FRIEND 1	you ain't asthmatic

FRIEND 2	fuckinhell my chest!
FRIEND 1	Your chest.
FRIEND 2	My *chest*!!
FRIEND 1	Your / chest.
FRIEND 2	This is what 'right' feels like this is what bein right feels like *fuck* this shit hurts –
FRIEND 1	you'll be –
FRIEND 2	bein right hurts no one tells you that bein right is painful truss mi – if this is what bein right feels like – hueeeeurrrghh!! I dun a difference. I made a difference. I did I did IdidIdid –
FRIEND 1	I saw
FRIEND 2	who / woulda – ?
FRIEND 1	(I) saw you done / somethin.
FRIEND 2	Who woulda thought?!
FRIEND 1	I saw you done somethin / that –
FRIEND 2	I didn't even know I didn't even know y'know – only went –
FRIEND 1	only went cos –
FRIEND 2	only went cos –
FRIEND 1	(you) only went cos I / said.
FRIEND 2	only went –
FRIEND 1	cos I told you
FRIEND 2	only went cos –
FRIEND 1	(you) only went cos you ain't never been before and started to feel bad that you was missin somethin missin out on somethin that everyone else was goin, had been goin, have been goin to. From time.
FRIEND 2	I –

FRIEND 1	started to feel left outta somethin wanted to feel right in somethin so went / on –
FRIEND 2	hold up – I –
FRIEND 1	went on it cos I was on you about it after all the times I been. After all the times I went. After all the times I been and went, without you. From day.
FRIEND 2	…Everyone in their own time ennit.
FRIEND 1	You're late.
FRIEND 2	…You told me everyone in their own / time.
FRIEND 1	I gave you shit to watch – you watch it?
FRIEND 2	
FRIEND 1	Gave you things to read thass stayed / unread.
FRIEND 2	Like you know
FRIEND 1	invited you to –
FRIEND 2	how you do / you –
FRIEND 1	from time I been askin / and –
FRIEND 2	you do-you how you do-you, yeah? And I'll do – me 'in my own time' you said – *you* said. Or ain't you sayin. Now.
FRIEND 1 FRIEND 2	
FRIEND 1	You read what I gave you to read?
FRIEND 2	Never knew there was no timetable.
FRIEND 1	Didju?
FRIEND 2	Never knew it was on the clock.
FRIEND 1	Didju read what / I – ?
FRIEND 2	Whatever.
FRIEND 1	You watch what I give you to watch?

FRIEND 2	
FRIEND 1	You see what I WhatsApped, what I shot, what I showed, what I exposed what I spat out on social (media)?
FRIEND 2	
FRIEND 1	You watch what I risked while I stood there and stood there and stood there witnessin' and recordin the Sista shoutin from across the way with a four-a-them and the one-a-her –
FRIEND 2	yeh / I
FRIEND 1	four-a-them in uniform and one-a-her – you / watch –
FRIEND 2	I do / know.
FRIEND 1	you watch that you watch *that*?
FRIEND 2	Saw / some –
FRIEND 1	Any a that? Alla / that – ?
FRIEND 2	saw some / shaky –
FRIEND 1	Didju even bother?
FRIEND 2	
FRIEND 2	Saw some shaky somethin – a few seconds of some shaky footage shot from far, su'un in the distance – tried to see what that was but y'know – it bein shot from so far back was hard to tell what-the-fuck was goin on. But saw you – heard you complyin with the 'Move along' complyin with the 'There's nothin to see here' with the 'Switch that off', then it snapped off – it was snapped off, you shut your shit little effort of filmin off as soon as they said. As soon as they said. Saw that. Saw that, brief brief encounter as you switched up, switched off and…

FRIEND 1	
FRIEND 2	
FRIEND 1	…I'm the one always been goin –
FRIEND 2	ooooohhhh
FRIEND 1	knowing the history of –
FRIEND 2	right
FRIEND 1	knowing why I'm supporting / it.
FRIEND 2	(*Dry.*) right on. Didn't know you had to take an exam before you / can –
FRIEND 1	You never even came to –
FRIEND 2	we all know why you go
FRIEND 1	you never come to / any –
FRIEND 2	everyone knows why *you* go, always tellin everyone you're goin
FRIEND 1	'always', yes, on the regular, yes, large or small hot or cold, near or / far –
FRIEND 2	martyring your way to marchin
FRIEND 1	convenient or inconvenient cause after cause time after / time
FRIEND 2	we all know 'bout *you* –
FRIEND 1	I know why I'm there.
FRIEND 2	I know why / I'm –
FRIEND 1	You – y'there for two minutes and –
FRIEND 2	what?
FRIEND 1	
FRIEND 2	
FRIEND 2	What?
FRIEND 1	
FRIEND 2	The two minutes I'm there I dun more'n you in your two years attending and

flyering and watching and talkin and
marching and… achievin fuck-all for all
the fuckin causes you cling to. But bein
seen to be there.
Achievin', shit-all.
I dun somethin.

FRIEND 1

FRIEND 2   Made a difference. Made a mark.

FRIEND 1   Made / somethin.

FRIEND 2   Least I did that.
Cos if I'd,
'became unwell'
I'd want me marchin for me more'n you.
Someone like you. What – ? Nah.

If they did me like they done her
did to me
what they done to her
I'd want someone like me marchin.
I'd want someone like me
filmin.
I'd want someone like me
'witnessin'. Basic.

…Didju even see?

FRIEND 1

FRIEND 2   Didju even see what I did-what I dun?

FRIEND 1

FRIEND 2   Had the courage to do.

FRIEND 1

FRIEND 2   Did you even…?

FRIEND 1

FRIEND 2   Or you was standin at the back busy lookin
pretty or su'un?
Maybe you couldn't see – standing so far
back maybe you couldn't see nuthin –

FRIEND 1	(*Quietly.*) fuckin / hell.
FRIEND 2	from the safety of bein behind someone, someones, loads a someones. Back-a-the-crowd. Back-a-the-bus. Inconspicuous. Ineffective. Mebbe you had your head in a book on how to march while I was busy up front doin it. (*Dry.*) Butchu can say you was there. To all and everyone who you love tellin, least you can say that. Again. Count it off notch it up march it out.
FRIEND 2 FRIEND 1	
FRIEND 2	You look forward to it –
FRIEND 1	(*Dry.*) right.
FRIEND 2	You look forward to marchin – at the back
FRIEND 1	(*Dry.*) right
FRIEND 2	bit of a day out for you defining you
FRIEND 1	fuck / off.
FRIEND 2	but if it was me not comin outta no cell – or comin outta some cell wrong, fuck me, I'd want more'n day trippers waving a flag and chanting some collective shit of shallowness, or hashtagging some bullshit of outrage that is forgot before the next post-of-fuckery. I'd want somethin more'n that. A bit more'n that. If it was / me.
FRIEND 1	But it ain't you. Is it – iss not about you. Is it.
FRIEND 2	
FRIEND 1	(*Dry.*) Somethin ain't about *you*.
FRIEND 2	Iss about 'all of us' ain't it?
FRIEND 1	Oh fuck / off.

FRIEND 2	You got marchin envy or summink? (You) got protest pride is it? Me goin trigger su'un in you – y'green-eyed marchin monster comin out now is / it?
FRIEND 1	(*Quietly.*) From a two-minute-fuckin-marcher –
FRIEND 2	what?
FRIEND 1	
FRIEND 2	No what?
FRIEND 1	
FRIEND 1	(*Dry.*) I'm glad you had a good time.
FRIEND 2	Weren't about havin no 'good time' was it –
FRIEND 1	(I'm) glad you enjoyed / yourself.
FRIEND 2	not about havin a – as you keep sayin kept sayin, so I ain't sayin I had a good-time-nuthin cos thass been made clear thass wrong – that that'd be wrong. You've made it crystal that no enjoyment is to be had, made that very –
FRIEND 1	glad you enjoyed y'self got yourself seen
FRIEND 2	I dun –
FRIEND 1	(*Dry.*) down the front and 'dun somethin'… yeah. You've said. You did. Take a selfie while you was doin it didja?
FRIEND 1	
FRIEND 1	Didju?
FRIEND 2	…I was up the front
FRIEND 1	did you?
FRIEND 2	
	FRIEND 1 *laughs a little, dry.*

FRIEND 1	And you weren't up front. People had stepped back.
FRIEND 2	Leavin me up front on my ones / and I –
FRIEND 1	People stepping back don't mean you stepped up
FRIEND 2	I was left up the front stayed up front and did my bit. Which is the same as steppin up – or have you got a leaflet somewhere sayin it ain't that or some list of rules of how shit should be done or-or a black-and-white documentary longer-than-fuck sayin that don't mean nuthin and that don't matter? Cos me doin my little bit looks like iss a little bit more'n you an' whatever-the-fuck-you-was-doin. Not doin. At the back… Again. Film some of it on y'phone didja?
FRIEND 1	You –
FRIEND 2	while you was busy stepping back –
FRIEND 1	I –
FRIEND 2	while you / was –
FRIEND 1	where was I? Where was I? Havin y'head so far up y'arse for so long lookin at y'self you didn't have time to look for me or for no one else – y'don't know where I was. It was a march.
FRIEND 2	I marched.
FRIEND 1	It was a protest.
FRIEND 2	I protested.
FRIEND 1	It was a *demonstration*
FRIEND 2	I did that. (I) did that I did that. And then some. Didn't I.

Scene Six

US.
The same SON *and* MOM *as in Scene One.*

DAD	…It means can mean means that something will miss you. Someone. Will miss you. Miss you hard. Harder than that.
MOM	I would.
DAD	Yes. Would miss you. I'd miss you Son.
SON	
DAD	Yes.
MOM	Yes.
DAD	…But that's not the point.
MOM	(*Quietly.*) Yes.
DAD	That doesn't matter.
MOM	No.
DAD	It means of value. 'Of value'
SON	I am –
MOM	yes you are.
SON	I / am.
DAD	You are. You are to us Son.
MOM	*Yes.*
DAD	But you're not.
MOM	…It means, of worth
SON	same as value –

DAD	not to them
SON	'of worth' fits.
DAD	Should fit
SON	am I?
DAD	You are
MOM	know you / are.
DAD	you are more valuable than I could think, than I have thoughts for. Than I can bear to think.

SON *smiles*.

MOM	It means… that it would be meaningless without you here
DAD	I would be meaningless without you here. Your momma would be meaningless without you here.
MOM	Your daddy, couldn't, wouldn't, without you here.
DAD	I love your being I love you being / here.
SON	I love being / here.
DAD	I can't remember when you weren't
MOM	life wasn't as, before you was
DAD	my life was just is, before you was, now it's as good as, with you in it
MOM	hasn't been and wasn't this as-good-as, before you were in it.
DAD	You grew me, much as we grew you, Son.
SON	
DAD	Thass how much.
MOM	(*Quietly.*) But thass not / the point.

DAD	If you weren't here it would be a sorry difference yes a crippling difference
MOM	yes
DAD	an indescribable difference a crushing difference an unbearable agonising excruciating horrendous unspeakable difference, if you weren't here, Son. …But that's not the point.
SON	
DAD	I'd miss you.
SON	Dad
DAD	your mom would miss you
MOM	but. Me missing him doesn't matter, wouldn't / matter.
DAD	us missing you wouldn't matter wouldn't be the… We're not the point.
DAD	
DAD	…It means – can mean, substantial. You are *substantial*
SON	thank you / Dad.
DAD	you are. But you're not.
MOM	(*To* DAD.) You are. But you're not.
SON	(*To* DAD.) You are. (*To* DAD.) Get it from you.
MOM	(*To both*.) You are. But you're / not.
DAD	Substantial isn't invulnerable
SON	you are.
DAD	Substantial isn't invincible

SON	you / are.
MOM	Substantial shouldn't have to be
SON	(*To* DAD.) you are / Dad.
DAD	Shouldn't have to be but it has to be
MOM	shouldn't need to / be.
DAD	substantial isn't unshakeable
SON	you don't / shake.
DAD	you shouldn't have to be unshakeable, Son.
	But you should.
SON	Dad –
DAD	substantial isn't enough
SON	Mom I –
MOM	won't be enough – itmeansitmeans it means it / means –
DAD	you mean the world to me, youmeantheworldtome youmeantheworld tome you mean the world to us.
SON	…And the world?
MOM	In this world?
SON	
DAD	This side of it… You don't.
MOM	It means –
DAD	it means, loved. Loved. You are so loved
SON	I am
MOM	you are
DAD	more than the / world.
SON	I –
DAD	more than this world could / know.

SON	Dad I –
DAD	more than this world could offer more than this world owes you.
SON	And in this world?
DAD	You are not.
SON	
DAD	…I love you.
SON	I know. I –
DAD	but you're not.
SON	I love –
MOM	I know Son but you're not.
DAD	You are. But you're / not.
SON	I love you Dad
DAD	I wouldn't want to be here without you.
SON	(I) love you Mom
MOM	(I) couldn't be here without / you –
DAD	couldn't stay in this world without you in it – .
SON DAD	
SON	(*Quietly.*) …Not the point…?
SON MOM	
MOM	(*Quietly.*) No.
DAD	…No. No. Not the point. No.
	Beat.
SON	(*Quietly.*) …Dad.

DAD

SON   Dad?

DAD   ...Son?

SON   What did you do with your hands?

Scene Seven

US.
The same characters as in Scene Four.

YOUNG ADULT   …I ain't a-one to –

ADULT   you still talkin?

YOUNG ADULT   …I ain't a-one to, to siddown and sing
about it.
Is all.

ADULT

YOUNG ADULT   Is all I'm sayin.

ADULT

YOUNG ADULT   I ain't someone to march till I drop
about it.
I know petitioning and politicking does
fuck-all for it.
I ain't gon' hashtag it.
I ain't gon' Instagram it.
I ain't a-one to kneel in prayer about it
I ain't a-one with your patience for it –
waitin on their timetable for it – nah –
progress is a bitch yeah? Progress is a slow
bitch with a wandering mind that drags her
bare feet
but
change kicks ass
change don't give-a-fuck
change gon' do its thing with or without
you.
Change ain't waitin on no permission
no one's permissions
change changes before you
before you even know how or why
then iss already moved the-fuck-on.
Change is somethin thass *done* – gets shit
done 'progress' meanders, wanders,
languishes, strolls fuckin… *dawdles*.

Change fucks. Shit. *Up*.
(Change) kicks 'progress's' ass
drop-kicks 'slow'
slaps up 'excuses'
fuckin wid progress's failures on the way
and-and I got shit I wanna do but they
make it that I can't do it till I force their
shit to change to let me do what I should be
doin anyway.
I got – normal shit everyday regular shit –
but they taking my time, takin up my time
– makin theyselves take my time. (I got)
shit I wanna feel but they takin my
attention takin up my attention like a – .
I'ma change shit cos I *gotta* change shit –
gotta change this shit ain't got no choice.
I'ma change *somethin* –

ADULT   anythin ain't 'somethin'.

YOUNG ADULT   I wanna – see-cos – we ain't doin like you
                 –

ADULT   you ain't me

YOUNG ADULT   we ain't like you –

ADULT   you ain't / me.

YOUNG ADULT   you liked to be liked –

ADULT   no / it –

YOUNG ADULT   you wait to be liked waited to be liked –

ADULT   you know what / we – ?

YOUNG ADULT   we don't give a shit

ADULT   can tell / that.

YOUNG ADULT   we don't give a –

ADULT   (thass) the problem

YOUNG ADULT   you wanted to bring-along

ADULT   now you soundin younger than you / is.

YOUNG ADULT   I'll ride –

ADULT   stupider than you is

YOUNG ADULT   I'll ride this shit alone
you wait for respectable – change ain't
fuckin polite, scuse my language – we still
havin to have the damn 'talk'. We still
havin to work round the fuckin basics, their
basics their base behaviours – what the
fuck do I even do wid my – ?!

He gestures his hands.

Really??

ADULT

YOUNG ADULT   I am your sons and them are still them and
them is still taking liberties still takin mine.
How is what they got *still* not enough? And
I respect y'shit thatchu did – even tho it
don't sound like I do – butchu need to
respect and accept the fact that it failed.

ADULT *goes to speak.*

You failed.

ADULT *goes to speak.*

With all due (respect) – they don't wanna
change they don't wanna *be* changed. So
let's start from there.

Give me a reason to not.

Scene Eight

UK.
Black British.

SON	If I put my hands up –
MUM	a threat, threatening.
DAD	
SON	Slowly?
MUM	Provocative.
SON	Showed my palms / then?
MUM	Inflammatory
DAD	(*Quietly.*) fuck
MUM	could be.
SON	…What if I raised my hands just to –
MUM	no
SON	to just –
MUM	no
SON	Dad?
DAD SON	
SON	If it was only –
MUM	aggression
SON	but just to show that they're –
MUM	an act of aggression.
SON	But –
DAD	(*Quietly.*) fuck
MUM	that won't work
SON	but
MUM	that won't work Son.

SON	Dad?
	If I left them down then – ?
MUM	Belligerent.
DAD	
SON	By my side – ?
MUM	Attitude
SON	what?
MUM	Attitude.
DAD	(*Quietly*.) Fuck.
MUM	To them.
SON	What if they were in pockets – in my pockets – Dad, I juss put 'em, leave 'em in my / pockets?
MUM	Concealing
SON	huh?
MUM	Concealing
SON	how?
	DAD *shakes his head*.
MUM	Obscuring
SON	what?
MUM	Cocky
SON	Mum, hands-hands together / then?
MUM	Don't matter / Son.
	DAD *shakes his head trying to hold his temper/keep it together*.
SON	My hands *together* – ?
MUM	(*To* DAD.) Tell him.
DAD	
MUM	Tell him.
DAD	

MUM	Tell him it doesn't – you gonna tell him somethin – ?
DAD	I'm –
MUM	you gonna help or are you just going / to –
DAD	I'm trying to –
MUM	'trying to' I'm trying to but I'm 'trying to' by *saying* somethin
DAD	I've said / something.
MUM	'fuck fuck and shit' isn't exactly 'something' isn't exactly helping isn't saying much of / anything.
DAD	So your kind of 'helping' is – this kind of helping / is – ?
MUM	We can all do a you but I'm telling him something – we agreed we would – we agreed we would *have* to tell him / something.
DAD	I know
MUM	'you know'
DAD	I would know I do know don't I? I'm trying I'm *trying* to – but how you're going at it how you're going at / him –
MUM	Me. (*Dry.*) Leave it to me. It's on / me –
DAD	you doing all the talking you doing all / the –
MUM	and I'm not 'going at him' and I'm doing all the talking cos you / aren't.
DAD	talking like that talking to him like that
MUM	we agreed
DAD	I agree – I know we *agreed* I agree – but not like this not like / that.
MUM	how would you do it? How would you say it – how was it said to you?

DAD	
MUM	Like this?
DAD	
MUM	You told me you got told like / this.
DAD	You finished? Cos I'll talk to our son and let him know –
MUM	tell him then tell him somethin / cos I'm –
DAD	I'll let him know what I want to let him know, *how* I want to let him know – and you're what?
MUM	
DAD	Yeh. Exactly.
MUM	Oh fuck off.
SON	Mum – ? Dad – ?
MUM	(*To* DAD.) You said –
SON	my hands (*Gestures together.*) – ?
MUM	(*To* DAD.) You said we'd – .
SON	My hands together?
MUM	(*To* SON.) Sarcastic – (*To* DAD.) tell him –
SON	but
MUM	(*To* SON.) mocking – (*To* DAD.) tell him *something*
SON	but
MUM	cynical
DAD	but
MUM	challenging
SON	but
MUM	provocative
SON	*but* –
MUM	to them.

MUM	
SON	
SON	
DAD	
SON	Dad…?
DAD	
SON	…Holding hands-holding hands –
MUM	you'd think.
SON	So?
MUM	No.
SON	No?
DAD	No.
MUM	See. (*To* DAD. *Dry.*) Great.
SON	So…?
DAD	No.
MUM	(*To* DAD. *Dry.*) Thanks. Well done.
SON	So?
MUM	Collusion, complicity
DAD	God
SON	behind my back then –
MUM	arrogance insolence ignorance
DAD	God this / is –
SON	but-but –
MUM	defiance.
DAD	(*quietly*) Fuck. This. Shit.
	MUM *nudges* DAD.
	'…Defiance.'
MUM	See.
SON	Gesturing that I –

MUM	aggressive
SON	but just that I –
DAD	aggressive
SON	if only I –
DAD	aggressive
MUM	antagonistic. See.
SON	
SON	…If I say somethin
MUM	too loud
SON	juss normal
MUM	too loud
SON	if I speak quiet
MUM	too loud
SON	if I question
MUM	confrontational
SON	if I reason
MUM	confrontational
SON	if I… If I…
SON MUM SON DAD	

SON *thinks hard.*

SON	If I look….

MUM *watches him.*

If I look at them – confidently look at /
them.

DAD	Yes.
MUM	Confronting.

DAD	Yes
MUM	no
DAD	yes
MUM	no / no
SON	but if I look away –
DAD	no
SON	but if I look away –
DAD	we didn't raise you to look away
SON	but if I –
DAD	you don't avoid lookin at nuthin, y'don't not look at nuthin, you don't look away Son, you don't avoid lookin at nobody, not no, body, you don't look at the floor you don't look down you don't avert your gaze. We ain't raised you to do that. To be that.
SON	…But if I –
MUM	guilt. Guilty aggressive aggressive aggressive subversive –
SON	then –
DAD	no.
MUM	No.
SON	Then –
DAD	no.
SON	Then what do I…? What do I even – ?

SON *thinks*.

Then-then…

He looks to his MUM, *he looks to his* DAD.
His DAD *is struggling.*

Scene Nine

US.
Same characters as in Scene Four and Seven.

ADULT
ADULT

YOUNG ADULT   Your silence is… I'm takin your silence as
                you – .

ADULT

YOUNG ADULT   I'ma take it as –

ADULT   my silence is not – .
                I'm choosin if my words – which words is
                worth it on you.

YOUNG ADULT

YOUNG ADULT   (*Quietly.*) Now you mad at me.

ADULT   (*Mad at him.*) I'm not mad at you.

                Beat.

YOUNG ADULT   Now you mad – .

ADULT   C'mon.
                No.

                Beat.

YOUNG ADULT   …Then.
                …I'm takin your silence as you struggling
                to see why I shouldn't cos y'hardly givin
                me any reason / not to.

ADULT   (*Quietly.*) It won't solve the situation /
                that –

YOUNG ADULT   Huh – what?

ADULT   And my silence is *my* silence, not your
                version of what my silence is and you doin
                whatchu don't even know you wanna do
                won't solve / the –

YOUNG ADULT   Didn't mention solutions did I? (I) asked for
                a *reason*. To not do, it. For me to not be, it.
                Of which I ain't heard one.
                Not one good one.
                From you.

ADULT   It –

YOUNG ADULT   in your 'silence'.

                ADULT *eyeballs him.*

                I ain't said I'ma solve shit I look like I'ma
                solution? I don't look like a solution I know
                that – but I'ma do my difference in a small
                way yeh, yeah whatever. Thass somethin.

ADULT

YOUNG ADULT   Thass something ain't it?

ADULT

YOUNG ADULT   That'd be – .

ADULT
YOUNG ADULT

YOUNG ADULT   …Cos you'd be doin what?
                To help. How?

ADULT   It –

YOUNG ADULT   sittin there lookin sorrowful?

ADULT   Say that *again*.

YOUNG ADULT

YOUNG ADULT   …I done wid sorrowful.
                Is all I'm sayin.
                Done wid pitiful.
                Is what I'm meanin.
                Done wid pity.
                Long-time.

                I take out the one who could be the father
                of the one who could be the father of the
                one who takes out the son of yours that

could be the son of your son.
I take out *that* father-of-the-father and
history's better for it and your son-of-your-
son could be the real change maker. The
real game-changer.
Revolutionary.
So I coulda played my part in a little way
with a big repercussion that could then be –
could have been, a big good thing done. A
really mutha-fuckin-big-change in a small
way. In a-one small action. That small
action. My action.
Thass all that / I'm sayin.

ADULT   You won't know who the father-of-the-
                 father –

YOUNG ADULT   neither do / you.

ADULT   or the mother-of-the-mother or the child-
                 of-the-child would or could / be.

YOUNG ADULT   Neither do you

ADULT   so you're losin your own

YOUNG ADULT   the risk of bein right is a risk worth takin.

ADULT   You losin your own argument before you /
                 even –

YOUNG ADULT   I ain't said I ain't never been wrong – ain't
                 never gon' be wrong, but changing
                 somethin is better'n doin nuthin.
                 Ain't it?

                 Ain't it.

                 Beat.

ADULT   …It-it would be in cold blood.

YOUNG ADULT   It's fire with fire.

ADULT   Give you sleepless nights

YOUNG ADULT   can't sleep now

ADULT   it won't, look good for / the –

YOUNG ADULT	how is this lookin now? How is *this* lookin good / now?!
ADULT	You're-you're better than that.
YOUNG ADULT	No. Nope.
ADULT	(It) would bring a backlash –
YOUNG ADULT	(*Dry.*) cos we don't got that
ADULT	more of a / backlash.
YOUNG ADULT	I'm juss lashin back the backlash lashin me
ADULT	you're –
YOUNG ADULT	I'm provoked –
ADULT	it would bring –
YOUNG ADULT	have been / for –
ADULT	it would –
YOUNG ADULT	for centuries and the 'backlash' lashes back at the drop of a hat-their drop of their hat / don't it.
ADULT	It would… It would…
YOUNG ADULT ADULT	
YOUNG ADULT	(*Quietly.*) C'mon. Come on. Gimme a reason to not. *Beat.* *Please.* *Beat.*
ADULT	It wouldn't work.
YOUNG ADULT	…But… This ain't working. Is it.

Scene Ten

US.
Same character from Scene Two.

YOUNG WOMAN   Lemme say it again premier, primero, først –
Danish baby – *first* – top of the damn class!
Them symbols, numbers, equations and
funny-lookin somethins everybody thinks
is over-hard – are under control and is my
thing.
Breakin shit down, workin shit out, aspects
into elements – rudiments, fundamentals,
them elements into molecules – particles,
atoms, then those atoms into –
and I been told I gotta not slip
gotta keep up – keep it up
been said iss expected of me,
said not in a pressurised oppressive parent-
teacher way... but in a sort of passively
pressurised oppressive parent-teacher way,
Dad did say don't bother come home if you
ain't got what you're capable a gettin. He
funny like that. Jokes.
I think.

I focused.
Cos thass comin from the man who ain't
had nuthin but built himself up to somethin
who I look up to as everythin.
And when I brought back
my high marks from my hard work – what
that brought to my daddy's face...

I ain't shy on it.
I put the work in.
I put the hours in.
Didn't do a world-a-fun-shit to stick with it
although me learnin the books was fun for
me – geek shit I know.
Head in books steada in the clouds

tho I'm the one who knows exactly what
those clouds is made up of,
ass in the library steada out and about
symbols, numbers, equations, atoms doin
they own sweet dance for me.
An' my gurls know not to mess wid me
when I'm on it, 'geeking out' – their words
not mine, know not to distract with their
'leave her to it y'all' as they leavin me to it,
the brothas know 'she gorn in' letting me
alone
and prouda me stickin with it.
So I knew
know

before we saw

what I felt when I felt what we felt…
That downwind tingle in my mouth
lips, tongue and taste changing
'we gotta step'
I thought
but the mood was still light
'we gotta step'
I say
but the mood is still tight
vibe still hype,
our points chanted
our outrage heard
our anger sang
crowds of us was us is us
beautiful,
numbers untold uncountable
beautiful,
collectively strong, loud and prouda-than-
proud a dark sea of us as far as anyone can
see.
And we pass the ol' woman thass always
out.
Always out first.
Lookin at us like we late.
Lookin at us like we ain't serious

and it is – *cold*
and this tingle in my mouth…
But we marching and marching
holdin on to each other
for collective heat
passin that same ol' woman in her thin
jacket who don't look like cold touches her.
Hardcore.
And we placard holding
holding each other, chantin
warm breath blowin into freezing cold air –
marching up our outrage.
But that downwind tingle in my mouth is
starting to…
'We gotta *move* people'
I drop it louder, get some turned heads
from my cold gurls,
questioning looks from the freezing brothas
givin me a
'Huh?'
whether they never hear or don't hear or
don't get it I get a too-late
'What?'
as the flashbang does iss job making
anythin else said unhearable
momentarily blinded by a light that ain't
holy
ears ringin in an impossible silence that
gets you wonderin if this is what deaf
sounds like…

Beat.

Till a next flashbang makes you know.
You ain't that.
Senses stunned.
Deliberate.
I see – kicking out from its canister, then
drifting like iss casual but ain't – the light
milky-white-cloud
drifting up and out.
Street level.

Our level.
Our direction.
Deliberate.
Downwind,
deliberate.
Deliberately done. By them.

In the less-than-half-second a silence
shouts and screams of us and our panic
follow
and this
casual cloud drift-of-drift tingling reaching
my mouth
then starts to
burn,
the burn intensifies
from my mouth down my throat – my
throat getting to closing – closing getting to
choking – I'm drooling like a baby.
Hearing, snaps back jarred back by my
hacking and choking and the hacking and
choking of us all, the shouts and screams
of us all –
I'm basically blind by that casual-white-
cloud thass still, drifting, drifting,
drifting…
Tears swelling racing falling swelling
racing falling swelling racing – not of
sadness or anger too sad for that too angry
for that but my body trying to flush out the
chemical irritant that is infecting them.
Like iss designed to. Like this is all meant
to.
It is designed to.
It is meant to.
It is working
as it should.
I would reach for water if I could reach for
my water but this shit is devised thatchu
can't.
Confusion.

And that ol' woman who been out here
before time, goes down.
My skin – burns.
It's meant to.
My nose burns.
It's meant to.
My throat on fire like inhaling raw flame
breathing hurts
breathing feels like you're not
breathing feels like you can't like you're
suffocating
that your throat is imploding
panic sets in –
all meant to
all deliberate
all designed.
Fired into and at.
To order. On an order. Calculated,
considered, intentional. Targeted.

*'Yo! Don't rub your eyes don't rub your
eyes y'all!'*

I yell – but am cut off by another
flashbanging spinning canister of
wickedness spilling its cloudy white
contents into the air before folks can heed.
The beautiful crowds of us scattering
vomiting crying panicking – scattering
vomiting crying panicking, placards
dropped chanting stopped, messaging
blocked, marching forgot protesting fucked
runnin runnin from the casual-white-cloud
into one another
then into another one
aimed at
fired at... just so.

Flashbang. Stun.

Black bodies staggering into each other
through that milky-white-cloud, red eyes
barely seein a watery half-nothin –

runnin the wrong way cos no right way can
be seen, as the storm-motherfucking-
troopers keep advancing barking at us to
'Clear the streets! Clear the streets!'
Knowing full-fuckin-well… we can't.

Chlorobenzylidenemalononitrile.

To those that didn't study them symbols,
numbers, equations and funny-lookin
somethins everybody thinks is over-hard…
To those that don't know they science
they chemistry
they physics.

Tear gas.

Is a motherfucker.

Scene Eleven

UK.
Black British.

MAN

Y'know…
When I sat in that cell
and sat in that cell
and sat in that cell.
And he come in stayin stood
tellin me what they could say to you.

When I was picked up and didn't know
why.
When they said I was
'bein aggressive'
and I weren't.
And I weren't.
When they said that I was shouting
when I was speakin.
I was speakin.
When they said I was actin aggressive
when I never was.
I never was
and then told to shut up when I asked them
what
'acting aggressive' is.

When they switched it to I was
'talkin aggressive'
then joked to themselves that we all sound
aggressive to them anyway.
When they said I was bein
'provocative'
and when I asked them
'how'
they said
'physically'
and when I asked them
'how – ?' when there's six of them and
one-a-me they said askin was provocative
and before I could say

'how?'
they said
'your mouth is gettin you into trouble so
best you shut up'.

When I asked them
'why me'
they smiled
'fits the description of'
and I knew I didn't and the description they
described was so shit, so shit, so shit –
again. It was laughable. Again.

When they said – the second-of-the-six –
that I was gesturing aggressively and my
palms raised in a passive (*Gestures 'how'.*)
and that second-a-the-six-a-them cuffed
them saying
'see. *See.*'

When they told me to stop speakin, so I
stopped speakin and the second-of-the-six-
a-them who had cuffed me smiled and
silent laughed then said my silence would
be used against me in a court of law.

When they challenged me to say somethin
and I said nuthin.
When they provoked me to say somethin
and I said nuthin.
When they mocked me to speak
I said nuthin
provoking me to get a reaction
said nothin
provoking me to get to reacting – I said
nuthin, they in my face – (I) said nuthin
said nuthin said nuthin said nuthin.
They darin me to say anythin to do somethin
to do anythin and when I still say nuthin they
challenge me, agitatin me, goading me,
taunting me, deriding my nuthin, mockin me
sayin-my-nuthin and when I didn't react to
anything they challenged me to do somethin,

challenge me to do somethin challengin me
to do somethin to say somethin to say
somethin and when I reacted
they said I was resisting arrest.

When they said my hesitation was
'obstruction'
when they dropped
'resisting arrest'
harder than they dropped me to the
concrete
sayin I'm
'making it worse for myself'
with their knees in my back – all five-of-
the-six… I couldn't think how much more
worse it could fuckin get. Then I did. Think
it.
Then it was. Worse.
In the back a the van.

…When they watched me when I
wouldn't,
then shouted again,
'Strip.
We told you to strip.'

When I wouldn't and didn't and the
second-of-the-six
not smiling now said that I would
how I would
how I will.
That I will.

I still wouldn't.

When I started to ask 'why'
the fifth-of-the-six sighed like I was stupid
turnin to face me like I was bein thick, the
second-of-the-six said again – not shoutin
now
but
quieter
and worse with it
'We're not gonna tell you again.'

Beat.

When I…

…When I started with my shirt

but before it was off they givin me the 'hurry up'.

When I slowly lifted my vest
they commentin that coulda come off wid my shirt.

When I untied my laces
third-of-the-six said I coulda slipped my feet out without doin the drama of the detail…

When I started on my socks
they swapped a look
with the second-of-the-six sayin
'We all know where this is goin so you might as well just hurry up and get on with it – .'

When my jaw tightened wid my hand on my belt
one-a-them seein smiled sarcastic sayin 'easy'.

Beat.
Beat.

When I'm standin in my boxers…

Beat.

Like a fuckin five-year-old…

Beat.

One-a-them says quiet
'This is harder for us than it is for you.'
Then smiles – to them not to me – like he's done he's part.

Beat.

When…
Then – .

Beat
Pause.

But…
So – .

Pause.

…'You can dress now.
(You can) get dressed now.

Thank you for your cooperation.'

(*Quietly.*) Juss like…
(*Quietly.*) Like it was (nuthin)…
Fuckin…

(*Quietly.*) Like it was fuckin…

He shakes his head, just..

(*Quietly.*) …Fuck…

Scene Twelve

US.
Same characters as before.

YOUNG ADULT	Idunsomethin Idunsumthin youseemedosomethin you see-me-do-the-damn-thing-I-dun??!! (I) dun somethin – lissen-lissen I dun-just-dun did / something –
ADULT	I / saw.
YOUNG ADULT	yousee yousee / yousee???
ADULT	I saw I saw / you.
YOUNG ADULT	Man!
ADULT	Could / see – .
YOUNG ADULT	Maaan! Didju see-didju hear?!
ADULT	I saw could see. Saw somethin. Heard something some / something.
YOUNG ADULT	Aarrgghhh man – !
ADULT	Looked real nervous –
YOUNG ADULT	*shit!* Man!
ADULT	I / know.
YOUNG ADULT	I-knew-I-knew-I-knew y'know iss a weird freakin feeling – I think this feelin is what a hundred per cent sureness feels – I think iss *that* – ain't never felt it before ain't never felt it about *nuthin* before ain't never felt it about no one before never felt so freakin sure before. *Real*. Iss real – .
	He draws breath – still hyped.
ADULT	
YOUNG ADULT	Iss like iss like – look at my hands look at my hands they're – can you see my hands?! Look / at –
ADULT	Can see your / hands.

YOUNG ADULT	shit!
ADULT	Adrenalin.
YOUNG ADULT	Damn –
ADULT	adrenalin
	He feels his own heart.
YOUNG ADULT	feelthatfeelthatfeelthatfeelthat –
ADULT	I can see – .
YOUNG ADULT	You can't see *feel* it – *damn* iss thru my chest pumpin like a fuckin – pardon my French – (I) could be havin a cardiac – I could be havin a / fuckin –
ADULT	You're not havin / no –
YOUNG ADULT	can you bring on a cardiac or su'un-?!
ADULT	You ain't havin no heart / attack.
YOUNG ADULT	My chest man my / chest!
ADULT	It ain't no cardiac / arrest.
YOUNG ADULT	You ever feel this youeverfeeldis – ?!!
ADULT	I've felt –
YOUNG ADULT	this is what 'right' feels like this is what bein right feels like damn this shit hurts –
ADULT	you'll be –
	He breathes heavily, catching breath but still full of adrenalin.
YOUNG ADULT	good hurts – a good hurt – a hard hurt but a – nobody tells you that nobody tells you that part that bein this right freakin hurts! Who / woulda – !
ADULT	I saw you done somethin.
YOUNG ADULT	Who woulda / thought?!
ADULT	I heard what you / done.
YOUNG ADULT	Didju see?!

ADULT	I –
YOUNG ADULT	Didju *see*?
ADULT	
YOUNG ADULT	Didju see?
ADULT	
YOUNG ADULT	(I) made a difference. Made a mark.
ADULT	Made somethin.
YOUNG ADULT	Made *my* mark.
ADULT	…Did somethin.
YOUNG ADULT	Didju even (see)?
ADULT	
YOUNG ADULT	Didju even see what I did-what I dun?
ADULT	Does it matter that I / do?
YOUNG ADULT	What I had the nerve to do.
ADULT	You there to be seen doin it or…?
YOUNG ADULT	
ADULT	You want me watchin you? You want an audience?
YOUNG ADULT	
ADULT	Or you do whatchu doin cos you know why you doin / it?
YOUNG ADULT	Couldju see, from the back?
ADULT	
YOUNG ADULT	Back-a-the-crowd. Back-a-the-bus. Back-a-the-line. Polite. Liked. That where you was? Again.

YOUNG ADULT ADULT	
YOUNG ADULT	Couldju see from there? See me from there.
ADULT	
YOUNG ADULT	Y'didn't even –
ADULT	I wasn't lookin for / you.
YOUNG ADULT	I toldju I would –
ADULT	wasn't there for you s'not about*chu*.
YOUNG ADULT	…Couldju see anythin from there? Couldju hear anythin from, back there? Again? Didju hear the: *'Yo! Don't rub your eyes y'all!'*? You hear that from way over from a Sista way over – from wherever you…? Did your eyes burn like mine did? Or was you too upwind while I was down of it? Did your throat start burnin like mine was? Or was you comfortably at the back backed up backed off? Again?
ADULT	
YOUNG ADULT	Was you rush-rinsing your eyes with water – any water stung by the evil clouds of fuckin – ? Or juss stood casually sipping yourn watching the carnage up the front that you couldn't really actually see, cos you so, so, far… *back*. Shit.
ADULT YOUNG ADULT	
YOUNG ADULT	And it ain't about me. But iss about me. Collective.

ADULT	Selfish.
YOUNG ADULT	Communal.
ADULT	Self-centred.
YOUNG ADULT	Empowerin.
ADULT	Egotistical.
YOUNG ADULT	...I was on point up front. Toldju I would be. Toldju I'd do somethin. Toldju I'd do somethin that matters. Do somethin to make a difference. And... me doin my little bit looks like iss a little bit more'n you an' whatever-the-fuck-you-was-doin. Have been doin. Not doin. At the / back.
ADULT	(*Quietly.*) It was a march.
YOUNG ADULT	Huh?
ADULT	It was a *march*.
YOUNG ADULT	Marchin days is over man.
ADULT	It was organised
YOUNG ADULT	which does what?
ADULT	It was a protest.
YOUNG ADULT	Protests fail.
ADULT	It was a *demonstration*
YOUNG ADULT	demonstratin what? Again? Again? Again? *Again?* They don't lissen. They haven't lissened. They don't want to and I ain't waitin no more to be heard. They ain't changed. They don't wanna change. Don't intend to. And I ain't waitin no more for them to bother.

                    I demonstrated – demonstrated
                    that these hands
                    my hands
                    don't fuckin play.

ADULT
YOUNG ADULT

YOUNG ADULT   Maan.

                    They offer crumbs
                    you want the slice…
                    You want a slice.

                    I want the fuckin pie.

80

PART TWO

Scene One

US.
An African American FEMALE, *a Caucasian American* MALE.

MALE – no, no, you misunderstand me. His father had left when he was twelve.

FEMALE Not eight?

MALE Not eight, twelve –

FEMALE oh.

MALE Which makes

FEMALE right

MALE makes all the difference.

He smiles.

FEMALE …I think aged twelve is old enough to –

MALE you haven't been through what he's been through.

FEMALE He hasn't been through what I've been through.

MALE You're not twelve.

FEMALE …When I was –

MALE I didn't –

FEMALE when I was / twelve –

MALE I didn't ask you about –

FEMALE I do remember / knowing –

MALE are we talking about you or are we talkin about him – you've come in here asking about you? Or-because I'm not your – if you / are.

FEMALE	I'm / not.
MALE	If you want to offload –
FEMALE	I've got no intention / of –
MALE	feel you need to offload about you
FEMALE	no-no
MALE	find out about you
FEMALE	no
MALE	I suggest you go / to –
FEMALE	I don't wouldn't haven't / and –
MALE	to-to some other –
FEMALE	I'm not –
MALE	this isn't that and I'm not –
FEMALE	no. And no.

Beat.

What he's been through isn't unusual isn't out-of-the-ordinary. Is what I'm say-trying to say. All I'm trying to / say.

MALE	It's outside of his 'ordinary', which makes it –
FEMALE	isn't as much as other / people's –
MALE	for him it makes it –
FEMALE	other people go through / much –
MALE	but we're not talking about other people. Are we? You're asking about him.
FEMALE	
MALE	Aren't you.
FEMALE	…Other people have out-of-the-ordinary experiences is all I'm trying to –
MALE	I'm talking specifics.

FEMALE	I'm being –
MALE	I don't know what you're being but if generic is your / thing –
FEMALE	I'm being-trying to be very –
MALE	if generic is your thing I can't – y'know that's not what I – and you'd be wrong.
FEMALE	But I'm being specific.
MALE	Are you?
FEMALE	
MALE	Are you.
FEMALE	I'm –
MALE	what, are you?
FEMALE	
MALE	Do you even know?
FEMALE	I-yes.
MALE	'I-yes' are you sure?
FEMALE	I / am.
MALE	Don't sound sure
FEMALE	I / am.
MALE	'I-yes' doesn't sound –
FEMALE	I am. Sure. And I am being 'specific'.
MALE	Yes, we are.
FEMALE	'…Twelve'
MALE	'twelve'. His father had left when he was twelve – aged twelve. Makes a difference. Developing years and all / that.
FEMALE	Not eight then.

MALE	Not eight / *no*.
FEMALE	No.
MALE	That's been-someone's said that wrong written that down wrong somewhere and it's been lazily repeated –
FEAMLE	it was –
MALE	you're lazily repeating it, like I've said. A male child –
FEMALE	a boy –
MALE	he is 'a boy'. Well observed well done
FEMALE	I –
MALE	almost teenage and-but y'know a father leaving is damaging in a boy. At twelve. Damage, damage / done.
FEMALE	But I think –
MALE	studies say the studies say –
FEMALE	but I think / that –
MALE	the studies say – and I didn't come to you to ask you what you thought, y'know – er, you've come here to ask me, I'm here – you're there. You came – I was here. Yes?
	He smiles.
FEMALE	…But the mother, the mother wanted –
MALE	y'know, with the absence of a (father) – not even absence in a passive way, if we're being accurate and talking detail in detail, the *leaving* of the – the activity-practical activity of leaving the family home – a parent leaving the –
FEMALE	but it was / amicable.
MALE	the leaving of the father from the family home around that / age –

FEMALE	It was very amicable –
MALE	for a child – the child-for a boy, for that boy – is dramatic.
FEMALE	There was very little drama.
MALE	Is traumatic
FEMALE	the kids testified they were comfortable with the situation.
MALE	It's not as bad for the adults – may not have been as bad for the adults but who knows, studies have shown –
FEMALE	the kids in the household said / that –
MALE	what I've told you – am telling-explaining, is that it was a... factor. It was – the studies say it was possibly a trauma to *that* twelve-year-old child
FEMALE	any / child?
MALE	*that* twelve-year-old boy –
FEMALE	any child / though?
MALE	*specifically*.
MALE FEMALE	
FEMALE	... But what about – ?
MALE	*Specifics*. Yes? Not difficult. Yes?
FEMALE	... No
MALE	what?
FEMALE	No.
MALE	No?
FEMALE	No. Sir.
MALE	'No'?
FEMALE	I think –

MALE	really – 'no'?
FEMALE	I think / that –
MALE	You've read what I've read?
FEMALE	I –
MALE	I'm sorry – you've studied what I've studied?
FEMALE	I –
MALE	you've got the – ? That I've got?
FEMALE MALE	
FEMALE	…No.
MALE	'No'. Thass a 'no', that's *the* 'no'.
FEMALE	Yes-no.
MALE	I welcome discussion-discussions I do and I / welcome –
FEMALE	Yes / no.
MALE	I do, am open and up for that but equally, I welcome people to admit when they're… yeh?
FEMALE	
MALE	Yes?
FEMALE	…Yes. / No.
MALE	About something. And I appreciate, I'd appreciate people here – who come in here asking whatever-it-is-you're-asking, to have read the studies and done your homework before they –
FEMALE	I / have.
MALE	before they – or if they don't know about (something) or have a lack of – . There's nothing wrong in that. In *admitting* that.

FEMALE	
MALE	In saying that.
FEMALE	
MALE	Hm.
FEMALE	
MALE	And. I know there's worse. I do know there's worse than what he may have –
FEMALE	he had sisters.
MALE	I do know that / but –
FEMALE	What about his / sisters?
MALE	and although not totally comprehensive
FEMALE	he had – has two / sisters.
MALE	the studies say – the studies do / say –
FEMALE	One older one younger both okay both normal.
MALE	'Normal.'
FEMALE	Yes and –
MALE	'normal' now that's a term
FEMALE	socially and as far as we – they're fine is what I / meant – .
MALE	'Fine', 'normal', now, are we going to have to –
FEMALE	what I mean –
MALE	y'know because those terms –
FEMALE	I know – . Yes
MALE	yes, do you?
FEMALE	Yes.
MALE	Hm.
FEMALE	Relative

MALE	very
FEMALE	I meant – what I meant –
MALE	I'm sure you did. There's a course for that, learning about that – those kinds of terms did you – ?
FEMALE	I don't have / to –
MALE	Have you – ?
FEMALE	I don't need to.
MALE	Well, y'know –
FEMALE	I don't – didn't don't need / to.
MALE	Y'think. Okay.
FEMALE	
MALE	Specifics. My point exactly. Your language –
FEMALE	I –
MALE	no.
FEMALE	…No.
MALE	An example, see?
FEMALE	
MALE	Important. And you're presuming I don't know he had sisters?
FEMALE	
MALE	Is that something you're presuming I didn't know, hadn't known wouldn't have known wouldn't have read, studied, questioned or asked?
	He smiles.
	Really?
	He watches her.

	I'm not underestimating you. I would appreciate it if you…
MALE FEMALE	
MALE	… Yes?
FEMALE	
MALE	Thank you. And-but with domestic violence thrown in –
FEMALE	there was no domestic violence.
	Beat.
MALE	With domestic violence in the mix –
FEMALE	there was no domestic / violence.
MALE	I'm just – with abuse of any / kind –
FEMALE	There was no abuse.
FEMALE MALE	
FEMALE	…Documented, or stated. Sir.
MALE	Well, we don't know, exactly.
FEMALE	Well… we do.
MALE FEMALE	
	She goes to speak but doesn't.
MALE	Abuse can take many forms.
FEMALE	She has said that –
MALE	DV takes many forms
FEMALE	said categorically there was no domestic / abuse.
MALE	we don't know what happens behind closed doors – what's 'normal' behind closed doors do we, do we? Not for sure.

FEMALE	She's said / no – .
MALE	And after years of –
FEMALE	the kids said no as well – the sisters I / mean.
MALE	and who knows what's said if it was that insidious psychological abuse taking place within that household, nothing 'documented' doesn't mean something doesn't exist. Doesn't mean people are going to be forthcoming doesn't mean it's going to be an easy admit, doesn't mean it's easy to admit that that was going on so if they did say nothing or said it didn't, doesn't mean that it did not take place. Does it?
FEMALE	…But it didn't.
MALE	Or are you speaking for them now?
FEMALE	
MALE	As well as for everyone else.
	He watches her.
	Y'know the studies, the studies done can be quite broad – are intended to be quite – narrowness doesn't / help.
FEMALE	There wasn't any domestic / abuse
MALE	narrowness of thought doesn't help
FEMALE	none.
MALE	Isn't / helpful.
FEMALE	The daughters-their daughters specifically testified to that / fact.
MALE	Maybe the father was good at it. And didn't let it show. Left no bruises left no marks.
	He smiles.

	Bit of an expert at it. Maybe. Maybe he was as good at what he did. As I am as good as what I do.
FEMALE	
MALE	Completely different – kind of – . Y'know, but – . Anyhow. We'll never know.
FEMALE	But we / do.
MALE	And an open – an open mind and an open attitude are vital. Critical. Crucial.
	He gestures to his head.
	In all areas of life. Important. Don'tchu think?
FEMALE	
	Beat.
	…The mom worked part time.
MALE	Now you're mumbling.
FEMALE	The mom worked part time as a 'supportive, loving home-maker', God-/fearing –
MALE	I am just here, you don't have to shout.
FEMALE	…Dad worked-the dad worked, three kids between them, all academically average, income average – or just above if it was a good year, economically stable, childhood sweethearts (that) married young-too young –
MALE	in your / opinion.
FEMALE	'drifted apart and separated amicably' –
MALE	I think if you read the / report
FEMALE	there's / nothing –
MALE	studied the studies –
FEMALE	and it's not 'my opinion' I've studied the studies it's in the / studies.

MALE	then you would see
FEMALE	there's nothing to / see.
MALE	see it how they see it.
FEMALE	I see it how I see it
MALE	which is –
FEMALE	and, the *husband* stated they were too young. Sir. The *husband* stated that 'they drifted apart / and – '
MALE	You seeing it how you're seeing it isn't necessarily seeing it right – you seeing it your way isn't necessarily –
FEMALE	I –
MALE	'fine'
FEMALE	what / I –
MALE	is it?
FEMALE	… What I'm trying to –
MALE	or have I gotta fall in with you so we can both 'see it' your way?
FEMALE	
MALE	Your 'right' way. Anything else. You want to state?
FEMALE	
FEMALE	… That I disagree I / disagree.
MALE	Got that. Think I'm capable of 'getting' that, my problem is – my problem with you / is –
FEMALE	I didn't come here to be a problem
MALE	my –
FEMALE	I didn't come here to be the problem, Sir.

MALE	Right. Well.
	He was – actually, still 'is' as he's
	incarcerated now, the son – not the
	husband, a damaged individual, a damaged
	young man, who did a damaging thing –
FEMALE	'damaging'
MALE	a young man doing a one-off act who had
	access – or gained access to firearms legally
	held in the house – his mother's house after
	the father had left, and who the 'mother' –
	ironically – and it's in the report –
FEMALE	I've read / it.
MALE	ironically said-says – said, she felt more
	secure with the family firearm being left
	with her for her-their / protection –
FEMALE	for / 'protection'
MALE	asked her husband – ex-husband to leave it
	with her and the licence details to be
	changed, as without an adult male in the
	house she felt her and the girls – and of
	course the son –
FEMALE	I've –
MALE	would feel more vulnerable. And would be
	– in their opinion – her opinion – they
	would feel more protected in case / of –
FEMALE	I've / read –
MALE	case of any unfortunate unforeseen event
	that took place such as a break-in or
	something – it's all there in / the –
FEMALE	I've read it.
MALE	Good.
FEMALE	I read it / all.
MALE	So it's ironic-it is ironic, then, that it's
	turned out so unfortunate

FEMALE   'unfortunate'

MALE   that these unfortunate unforeseen actions
                couldn't have been –

FEMALE   'unfortunately'

MALE   predicted. That she ends up being – . By
                the same gun she'd asked to keep in the
                house for protection

FEMALE   'un-fort-un-/ate'

MALE   he acted out his... a fantasist. Destructive
                one yes. But a fantasist. A one-off violent
                act by a young damaged 'fantasist' – by a
                boy who by all means had issues that may
                have been exacerbated by the leaving of his
                dad when he was twelve.

FEMALE   'Twelve.'

MALE   *Twelve*. Yes.

FEMALE

MALE   A fantasist. He's that.
                Specifically.

Scene Two

MALE	So of course, yes
FEMALE	that's a bag of planning right there.
MALE	Yes / yes.
FEMALE	That's pre-planned, premeditated – nothing spontaneous –
MALE	no no, yes.
FEMALE	Researched.
MALE	Nothing spontaneous, no
FEMALE	and this was before you could google your destruction of / choice.
MALE	I / suppose.
FEMALE	A lot of effort. By an adult – adults. Not an adolescent. Both adults. Not eleven –
MALE	are you / being – ?
FEMALE	not eight –
MALE	are you trying to / be – ?
FEMALE	This one went with a friend.
MALE	But he wasn't – y'know – they – I don't think he would have had their whole, y'know, they would have had their whole social circle –
FEMALE	*exactly*, they had a social circle
MALE	no one's saying they were popular –
FEMALE	people knew them, they knew people, individuals said they knew them –
MALE	but who really 'knows' who?
FEMALE	What?
MALE	Who really knows –

FEMALE	but –
MALE	who do you know?
FEMALE	What – ?
MALE	*Really* know, y'know?
	Beat.
FEMALE	…This isn't about me
MALE	this isn't about you no / but
FEMALE	so I wouldn't –
MALE	no but I was / just
FEMALE	who do you know? *Really* know then? Sir.
MALE	I – .
	He watches her. Smiles.
	…A lot of people want their time in front of a camera any camera saying how they know – 'knew' the-them. That's all I'm saying, that's the point I'm… yes?
FEMALE	
MALE	So me asking, 'who you know', who you think you know isn't me being – it's me backing up my own point. You understand.
FEMALE	
MALE	I don't really care what your answer is.
FEMALE	
MALE	I don't really care who you do or don't know.
FEMALE	
MALE	And your lack of an answer does, really, answer. Backing up my / point.
FEMALE	I know people. I know people.
MALE	I know people.

FEMALE	I really know people.
MALE	…Do you. They really know you?
FEMALE	This isn't about –
MALE	no it's not. But do they?
FEMALE	
MALE	It is about my point as I've / said.
FEMALE	Your people really know you then? Or you don't got no one to know you in the first place?
MALE	That's sounding personal.
FEMALE	Just trying to understand your 'point'.
MALE	Now that's just sounding, petty.

None of us actually know who knew them and how. Do we? And I don't trust anybody who jumps in on a vox-pop after the event saying how and when they… You get my point. Those that find a camera quicker than they find their sense and faster than they can string a sentence together saying how surprised they were at their actions and how wonderful they were as young men years ago and how they had loved their grandmas, helped old ladies across the road and cared for animals and all that – . Grinning into a camera enjoying their moment when it's not even – . You get the point. My point. Where I'm coming from.

Beat.

If he –

FEMALE	they
MALE	'they' had a large enough social circle someone would stop him-them, or say something or leak something or try to

	convince so, y'know I think my theory – the theory the studies stand
FEMALE	not if their social circle all thought like them.
MALE	Which would just make them all wrong. And being wrong – all being wrong / isn't –
FEMALE	My point.
MALE	All being wrong isn't the point. Isn't a point. In regard to his –
FEMALE	their
MALE	their social circle. Circles.

She watches him.

You could be 'wrong'.

Beat.

Your friends – if you have any – I'm not prying, could all be wrong.

He smiles.

A right-wing radical – *disaffected*, that's the –

FEMALE	no.
MALE	A *disaffected* right-wing radical –
FEMALE	no
MALE	with his friend, is the / point.
FEMALE	A hundred and twenty dead.
MALE	It's important to be accurate.
FEMALE	Eighteen / children.
MALE	Accuracy is an art, as are words. Important. And it was non-political, well, being pissed off with the Government isn't exactly political and would cover most of us…

A right-wing radical – both. Disaffected
right-wing radicals.
Specific. Specifics.
So, no.

FEMALE   No?

MALE   No.
A domestic home-grown act-of-violence on
a large scale, I'll give you that.
Unprecedented. I'll give you that. A home-
grown act-of-violence carried out by
right-wing radicals. *That*, yes. Specifically,
yes. Is what they were – are. Those two.
Yes.

Scene Three

FEMALE	So… this is where it / gets –
MALE	It's not complex.
FEMALE	…This is where it can start to get confusing to / me.
MALE	It's not confusing.
FEMALE	This is –
MALE	it's not confusing. The shooting of kids isn't confusing
FEMALE	they were high school by high / school –
MALE	kids shooting kids isn't confusing
FEMALE	and these ones weren't 'loners'. And they weren't 'poor'. And they weren't 'isolated' – when you looked into it. Not abused, not –
MALE	one of them was depressed
FEMALE	had got beyond eight or eleven years old which you seem to find so risky for your –
MALE	'twelve' and your sarcasm isn't helpful
FEMALE	I'm just making sure we've covered / all –
MALE	it's how you're –
FEMALE	no-no
MALE	yes-yes. It is.
FEMALE	I'm just trying to-not to –
MALE	no, you're not.

She watches him.

…One of them was struggling with – he, 'blogged', I think that's the term for – he 'blogged' it. Tho nobody seemed to be reading it, (he) seemed to have followers of exactly, two.

FEMALE	
MALE	Wrote his deepest and darkest. And there were some deepest and darkest. Depressed. And – obviously being depressed and being teenage can be a / difficult –
FEMALE	Depression is not an answer.
MALE	We're not doing / answers.
FEMALE	Depression is not an excuse.
MALE	I'm not giving excuses –
FEMALE	'teenage' isn't a good / enough –
MALE	I'm not giving excuses I'm giving reasons if you'd let me even – . Reasons they would give. Reasons that have been written down. Reasons that have been *studied* –
FEMALE	excuses
MALE	reasons that are in the studies. Teenagers shooting teenagers. Teenagers shooting their peers – and not 'excuses' / no.
FEMALE	Two armed teenagers shooting unarmed teenagers at their same / school.
MALE	One of them really was depressed. Probably clinical.
FEMALE	
FEMALE	And the other?
MALE	Y'know I think –
FEMALE	(he) was a bit sad was he?
MALE	I think you're not / being –
FEMALE	No-no I'm just trying / to –
MALE	I'm really starting to / think –
FEMALE	y'know really I'm just trying / to –
MALE	no it's not – and yes as I keep saying-trying to say – I don't know why you –

FEMALE	I'm just –
MALE	are you *are you* – 'just'? If you don't want to take this seriously I – if you can't take this seriously –
FEMALE	I'm takin / this –
MALE	I don't know why you're –
FEMALE	I'm taking this as seriously as / I –
MALE	why you're even here why are you here?
FEMALE	…I'm totally serious about this. Sir. But – .
MALE FEMALE	
FEMALE	'Teenage'…?
MALE	Disaffection.
FEMALE	Really??
MALE	The second follower he had on his blog was his friend, the only one they could find which was unfortunate as together they became – well. You know.
FEMALE	
MALE	The depths of disaffection can be destructive and –
FEMALE	'disaffection'
MALE	and coupled with
FEMALE	(*Dry.*) their young tender years…
MALE	
MALE	I can't take you – can't take this-you-if you're gonna – I mean – constantly going to be – you want to be taken seriously but you make *you* impossible to be taken / seriously.
FEMALE	I'm disaffected.

MALE	You're disaffecting.
FEMALE	Sir I –
MALE	what?
	Beat.
FEMALE	… You're saying 'teenage' is a factor –
MALE	yes.
FEMALE	Writing a miserabalist blog is a definition –
MALE	the studies / say –
FEMALE	being disaffected is a justification?
MALE	What I'm –
FEMALE	for you, all / those –
MALE	an aspect of those two specifically –
FEMALE	all those definitions afforded and-and, both male thass an / aspect.
MALE	no it's not.
FEMALE	Both from –
MALE	no it's not – those specific two individuals –
FEMALE	both –
MALE	not the issue –
FEMALE	both / are –
MALE	not the point not the issue not an issue and again, y'know if I can get a word in edgeways
FEMALE	I –
MALE	it's domestic, domestic is different and depression is mental health and mental health is a whole load of other issues right there.
FEMALE	I get depressed.
MALE	

FEMALE	I get depressed / but –
MALE	I think – and to make it personal isn't –
FEMALE	I don't load up, take aim and –
MALE	your disdain isn't –
FEMALE	I'm not / being –
MALE	if this is your way of trying / to –
FEMALE	I'm not being sarcastic I'm not showing (disdain) and I've come through teenage somehow managing not to massacre –
MALE	they aren't you.
FEMALE	I'm just –
MALE	they aren't / you.
FEMALE	they aren't me but me – we aren't allowed to / be them.
MALE	And are you are you?
FEMALE	What?
MALE	Depressed.
FEMALE	What?
MALE	Are you depressed, now…?
	Beat.
FEMALE	No. I'm… fulla joy.
MALE	
FEMALE	Having a great day.
MALE	
FEMALE	I'm fine but you see my point.
MALE	…No
FEMALE	the fact that / I –
MALE	actually no.
FEMALE	Mental health / isn't –

MALE	Are you or aren't you?
FEMALE	What?
MALE	
FEMALE	Having a good / day?
MALE	A depressive. Are you or aren't you that?
FEMALE MALE	
FEMALE	…Does that make a difference?
MALE	…No.
FEMALE	Does that make you feel / different?
MALE	No no.
FEMALE	Differently?
MALE	No. No no. No.
FEMALE	No?
MALE	No
FEMALE	'no'
MALE	no
FEMALE	yes.
MALE	
FEMALE	Yes. I am.
	Beat.
	And it's a bit of a bullshit argument –
MALE	I wasn't saying that it was / a –
FEMALE	excuse my language Sir, that you're – that they're trying / to…
MALE	I think you're-I think you're sort of taking what I say –
FEMALE	bullshit to try and make / that a –
MALE	what I was trying to say you're-y'know taking it out of – and using it out of

	context. And it's not helpful to make it personal and I didn't need you to disclose –
FEMALE	it's not personal and I didn't disclose I just made a / point.
MALE	disclosure is / personal.
FEMALE	I didn't 'disclose' anything I answered your question and made a valid point / that –
MALE	And personal gets emotional and neither are useful in this / context.
FEMALE	This is not me / emotional.
MALE	And as I've said – and I don't appreciate your use of bad language by the way – we're not here to talk about / you.
FEMALE	This is not me 'emotional'.
MALE	She said 'emotionally'.
FEMALE	
MALE	You are not the issue.
FEMALE	I'm not the / issue.
MALE	Your personal problems are your personal / problem.
FEMALE	I don't have –
MALE	so whatever personal-that personal –
FEMALE	haven't got / any –
MALE	that you have and I think *you have*, with all due respect, I think your personal is clouding / your –
FEMALE	it may, perhaps, I dunno, have been 'personal' to the seven dead schoolmates – students that their two 'peers' who armed themselves with semi-automatics, pipe bombs and a plan – I think *that* was very personal to those murdered.

MALE	
FEMALE	
FEMALE	Sir.
MALE	…I'm not saying they're not bad –
FEMALE	'bad'
MALE	or disaffected
FEMALE	'disaffected'?
MALE	Well –
FEMALE	'depressive'?
MALE	I'm not sayin they're not bad what they did wasn't (bad) – and yes one of them was- we've been over that and the other one was just plain old evil, put them together and we get – well, what we got. That. A depressive psycho – no offence – with a death wish and an evil young man with no moral compass, an absolute domestic, high-school, non-political disaster. A cultural phenomenon –
FEMALE	no
MALE	a teenage –
FEMALE	no
MALE	a cultural phenomenon that / can –
FEMALE	no
MALE	sometimes manifest itself within some teenagers
FEMALE	yours?
MALE	A cultural (phenomenon) – which is why it doesn't fit-isn't a neat fit which I feel is what you're looking for. A neat fit an easy fit an easy answer – a small word for a big subject but-so – no. Specifics. Yes? *Specifics*. Specifics matter. You and your personal issues don't.

Scene Four

MALE   Lone-Wolf.

FEMALE

MALE   Acting in isolation to – .

              She shakes her head.

              He acted alone, a Lone-Wolf.

FEMALE

MALE   It's a different kind of definition – .

FEMALE

MALE   Someone with no outside involvement or /
              influence.

FEMALE   Sounds like a bad eighties TV /
              programme.

MALE   Can you just – .

FEMALE   And he would have been influenced from
              somewhere from someone from some*thing*.

MALE   A lazy assumption.

FEMALE   Y'don't drop out of the womb armed with
              two automatic pistols and a semi-
              automatic –

MALE   he didn't use the semi-automatic rifle.

FEMALE   (*Dry.*) Well, we should be thankful for that
              I / guess.

MALE   It could have been worse, it could have
              been / worse.

FEMALE   Or maybe you do

MALE   what?

FEMALE   Maybe your – you – your (culture) do –
              does. Maybe you do drop out of the womb
              armed already – do the studies suggest you

| | do that – are that? Just born old evil out the evil old womb? |

He watches her.

Armed and ready bullets loaded before you've drawn your first / breath?

MALE	I mean I – y'know you don't help yourself.
FEMALE	This isn't about 'myself' as we've established as you've stated.
MALE	
FEMALE	Influenced.
MALE	Lone. Wolf.
FEMALE	*Influenced.*
MALE	
FEMALE	He had parents
MALE	we… don't blame the parents.
FEMALE	You don't blame the parents?
MALE	Not the parents.

She watches him.

FEMALE	He had family.
MALE	We don't blame the / family.
FEMALE	You don't blame the families?
MALE	You can't blame the families
FEMALE	you don't blame your / families – ?
MALE	The families aren't accountable for –
FEMALE	ours are. D'you blame their upbringing – ?
MALE	A Lone-Wolf may have psychopathic / tendencies.
FEMALE	D'you blame how-they-were or weren't raised or d'you presume they were-are just / all –

MALE	Specific psychopathic tendencies that may have been missed.
FEMALE	(*Dry.*) Mental health.
MALE	Well seeing as you're asking –
FEMALE	I wasn't / asking.
MALE	Asperger's – Autism one of those ones undiagnosed is suspected.
FEMALE	'Killer Autism'
MALE	on the spectrum and his –
FEMALE	semi-automatic automatic-pistol killer / Asperger's-Autism.
MALE	Are you going to – ?
FEMALE	I've got Asperger's.
MALE	
FEMALE	I've got –
MALE	have you?
FEMALE MALE	
MALE	*Have you?*
FEMALE MALE	
MALE	I don't quite… I don't quite get why you / are…
FEMALE	No. You don't do / you.
MALE	I'm just saying another aspect of why – and actually he came from a single-parent (family) Dad had left some time earlier –
FEMALE	you really do / find –
MALE	that study – would say in the study-studies, I mention again, possible / links.
FEMALE	you really do find words for everything. Words for anything –

MALE	the beauty of / language.
FEMALE	a totally fucking, bullshit world-of-words for nothin.
MALE	(*Dry.*) Thank You. Have you finished?
FEMALE	
MALE	…His act wasn't political. And, he may have had issues with his mother, it was his mother's gun – in fact he shot his mother
FEMALE	I know.
MALE	Unfortunate. And there's other factors
FEMALE	seventeen dead.
MALE	A psychopath
FEMALE	seventeen excluding his mother
MALE	yes
FEMALE	Nineteen including him – if you want to include him
MALE	well –
FEMALE	and her.
MALE	Well / if –
FEMALE	If he really matters.
MALE	Well-we-there was a marriage breakdown with his parents interestingly –
FEMALE	(*Dry.*) 'interestingly'
MALE	a possible / factor.
FEMALE	my marriage broke down.
MALE	This *isn't* –
FEMALE	and I didn't kill, feel to kill or have the urge to kill eighteen – seventeen strangers. Funnily enough.

MALE

FEMALE   Maybe I had the urge on occasion to hunt
              down my ex but that would be me making
              it too personal again. I / guess.

MALE   Your sarcasm doesn't work.

FEMALE   And that would be only one life.

MALE   And isn't welcome.

FEMALE   And the moment passed.

MALE

FEMALE   Eventually.

MALE

FEMALE   Maybe that was in my 'depressive' state.
              Maybe that was me being too 'emotional'.

FEMALE
MALE

FEMALE   …I'm fuckin with you. 'Lone-Wolf.'

MALE   Your language is really leaving a lot to
              be…

MALE
FEMALE

              Beat.

MALE   Dysfunctional, psychopathic tendencies
              undiagnosed –

FEMALE   he was / a –

MALE   a tragedy –

FEMALE   he was a –

MALE   a home-grown heart-breaking tragedy. He
              wasn't trying to change minds or-or change
              politics or-or, just a tragic – with possible
              mental health, y'know that Asperger's-
              Autism thing that has been mentioned –

FEMALE	you mentioned
MALE	along with access to a –
FEMALE	several
MALE	well, I'm not saying it's not a disaster it's a disaster. Was a disaster. A home-grown tragedy for all involved involving the Lone-Wolf young man.
FEMALE	People were terrified
MALE	I'll –
FEMALE	children / were.
MALE	I'll give you that 'terrified' is that part of the definition but that's as far as that goes. As close as it gets. He used a gun. Guns. The case is different. Slight. But different.

And he's… from here.

FEMALE
FEMALE

MALE   And do you?

FEMALE

MALE   Do you?

FEMALE   What?

MALE   Have Asperger's?

Scene Five

MALE	– and y'know some of them – who knows how many now really y'know they see it all played out in real time all over the – and God alone knows how many times with all the footage that's available everywhere on all (platforms) all the time, looped, replayed and relayed and y'know – .
FEMALE	
MALE	They sit there and watch it and drink it in and there has to be some – .
FEMALE	
MALE	And they – it has to go somewhere…
FEMALE	
MALE	What goes in has to come out.
FEMALE	
MALE	And I'm sure it does something to those susceptible few who as we've spoken about in the other categories – .

She watches him.

…I think – .

FEMALE	'Susceptible.'
MALE	Yes. I think – . The, what they see –
FEMALE	we all see
MALE	what they see is the – it's gonna sound, y'know and I don't mean to be inappropriate – .

She is bored by the conversation, he sees it.

The notoriety of-of the fifteen minutes of – I know it sounds like some old cliché or somethin but it's like a warped reality

	programme more warped than the warped reality programmes are or-or something – something that's… They are –
FEMALE	I know what they are.
MALE	They can't distinguish between what they see onscreen, they lose the distinction between… y'know? You know.
FEMALE	
MALE	… You're trying to minimise and simplify.
FEMALE	I didn't say / anything.
MALE	I'm trying to – but you're – before I even – .
FEMALE	
MALE	Hm.
FEMALE	
MALE	Copy Cats, the Copy-Cat phenomenon is what they / are.
FEMALE	'Copy Cats.'
MALE	It's a –
FEMALE	not a simplification at all. That.
MALE	It's a known –
FEMALE	not a dumb-down at all. 'Copy-Cat' killers. Warm and fluffy.
MALE	That's not / helpful.
FEMALE	You all have nine lives
MALE	you're not being helpful
FEMALE	I'm not here to be / helpful.
MALE	you have a talent for twisting what I – and no you're not and no I don't.
FEMALE	What?

MALE	Have 'nine lives'.
FEMALE	… You do and you don't even know it.
MALE	
FEMALE	… Are they – is there some weakness of mind that you – they – are allowed to / have?
MALE	I'm trying to –
FEMALE	are excused to have?
MALE	Why do you make this harder than it needs to be? Cos something like – comments like that really don't help
FEMALE	(*Dry.*) I'm not here to help
MALE	don't help *you*
FEMALE	I'm not –
MALE	you've *said*.
FEMALE	I'm / only –
MALE	I am trying to definitively and, precisely and, concisely have this –
FEMALE	I'm just trying to understand how / you –
MALE	have this / conversation.
FEMALE	how you persistently and consistently manage to *not* / say –
MALE	Y'know if I could finish if I could / finish – .
FEMALE	and keep a straight face while you're doing it.
MALE	If I could finish my point.
FEMALE	You'll finish your point
MALE	if you let me finish my / point.
FEMALE	When have you not? Ever. Not finished, your point.

	Beat.
	Beat.
MALE	…As I was saying, Copy-Cat –
FEMALE	ah fuck off.
MALE	
MALE	
MALE	…I think *you* have issues pertaining to you. I think you – as you have admitted have some (*Gestures to his head.*) that are unique to you that I don't need didn't and don't want to know about – and it's quite ironic – it is quite ironic that you brought up the word 'normal', coming from someone like… you.
FEMALE	I think-cos-sitting here hearing your painstaking 'details', your theories 'their' theories 'their' studies 'your studies' their 'reasons' your 'reasons' and following that shit through, I think, have come to think, am starting to conclude that you and your studies are full of fuckin shit. Sir.
MALE	How is this-you being like this helpful *at all*? I mean I don't – y'know – you ask me – come here and asked me – so I don't understand, I'm just trying / to –
FEMALE	(*Quietly.*) You wouldn't know where to start / with me. You wouldn't have enough bullets for me to have for me to use for me alone / to use on –
MALE	If you're not prepared to listen then – .
	Some – others, some are just, angry, / frustrated.
FEMALE	What have they got to be angry about?

	He exhales noisily, frustrated.
	You really want to start on, 'anger'? And, / justifications?
MALE	I'm sticking to the facts. You're starting to get –
FEMALE	depressed? *You're* depressing me that's for / sure.
MALE	sarcastic. I was going to say *sarcastic*, again.
FEMALE	Compared to (me) – what the *fuck* have you got be angry / about?
MALE	We are not here to talk about *you* and if you're not going to listen then… What's the point? What is the point?
FEMALE	Exactly.
MALE	… Y'know, you're coming across as quite angry, quite an angry… aggressive even – .
FEMALE MALE	
FEMALE	I – . Really.

Scene Six

FEMALE	You know this is bullshit?
MALE	Outrageous – yes. Heinous – yes. Violent – yes. Domestic – yes. Legal, a legal organisation doing illegal / things. Yes.
FEMALE	You do know that you're-that this – that what you're trying to, is actual – actually bullshit / right?
MALE	Sort of a group, more than –
FEMALE	in every office of every county, in every state in this country.
MALE	What you're –
FEMALE	bit more than a 'group'. Political.
MALE	What you're doing / isn't –
FEMALE	Bit more than 'political', structural –
MALE	you can keep trying to / talk –
FEMALE	bit more than 'structural' – social
MALE	talk over me all you want but what you're trying to say won't –
FEMALE	please fuck off.
MALE	Childish now. Are you, 'having an episode' of whatever that Autistic-Asperger thing you have is?
FEMALE MALE	
MALE	Did you ever get checked for that Asperger-Autism thing?

She watches him.

(*Dry.*) I can give you a number for somebody if you didn't.

She watches him.

Just trying to be – .

FEMALE	
MALE	
FEMALE	Organised.
MALE	…Being organised isn't a –
FEMALE	violent
MALE	in itself violence isn't a –
FEMALE	racist
MALE	a different conversation.
FEMALE	Religious
MALE	not a crime, you're confusing yourself
FEMALE	murderers.
MALE	You've answered your own question, a murderer is just that. Just that.
FEMALE	Multiple murderers.
MALE	Are just / that.
FEMALE	I mean I could go on – I think I will go / on.
MALE	Are you depressed again – are you one of the manic ones?
FEMALE	Supremacists.
MALE	I see what you're doing – trying to (do) but / no.
FEMALE	White supremacist white male –
MALE	no no. By their definition – you've just used their definition the clue's in their title –
FEMALE	murderous murdering –
MALE	you've said / that.

FEMALE	mass-murderers.
MALE	We can all list, y'know – not helpful.
FEMALE	Child murderers.
MALE	Well – yes, indiscriminate, but –
FEMALE	'indiscriminate'?
MALE	Indisc– well maybe that's not quite / the –
FEMALE	Maybe not 'quite'. No. Fucking no. Extremists.
MALE	…Depends where you stand on –
FEMALE	fanatics, fundamentalists –
MALE	this is just starting to feel like name-calling which / isn't –
FEMALE	*very* discriminate. Very precise. Very accurate. If we're going to use our definitions and this language, 'correctly'.
MALE	Now you're being –
FEMALE	*specifics*. I'm just
MALE	look / a –
FEMALE	specifics. (*Dry.*) And specifics matter. Right?

He watches her.

MALE	A-a home-grown domestic-vigilante racist organised subsection of society with religious leanings, yes. Their religious / leanings –
FEMALE	Bullets, bombs, burnings, hangings, lynchings, mutilations, shootings, destructions, defacing, torture, intimidations, abominations, perversions, organised, militarised, uniformed, hierarchical, vitriolic, ritualistic, political-death-cult-European-Protesteant-immigrant

-psychopathic white-sheet-wearing cross-burning motherfuckers.

MALE   …So – .

FEMALE   Terrorists.

MALE   …So… No. That.
                Wouldn't work. That definition –

FEMALE   terro/rists.

MALE   (That) definition doesn't work, it's quite simple / but you –

FEMALE   It is 'quite simple'

MALE   you just don't seem to –

FEMALE   I 'don't seem to' – ?

MALE   Don't seem to *want* / to –

FEMALE   I don't understand how you won't –

MALE   really, it's not something / to –

FEMALE   how you don't –

MALE   I know it can sound a little –

FEMALE   how you *refuse* to –

MALE   that it can sound a little / bit –

FEMALE   what is wrong with / you?

MALE   I'll give you that, that it can sound that little / bit –

FEMALE   With your Lone-Wolves, mentalists, your fantasists, your disaffected, your explicit fuckin excuses for / you.

MALE   It can sound a little bit hypocritical I know. A bit but –

FEMALE   you have words for you that are –

MALE   no

FEMALE   terrorists… Terrorists.

MALE   No. Y'know – .

FEMALE

MALE   It's not. We're not – .

FEMALE

MALE   It's not.

FEMALE

MALE   It's specific. *Specifics*.

FEMALE   What is *wrong* with you?

MALE   So.
              …It's not really hypocritical at all.

FEMALE
MALE

PART THREE

Scene One

US.

*Filmed: The following are from some Jim Crow Laws.
(Dates and places not always to be read.) The dialogue is
spoken/read direct to camera by American Caucasian actors/non-
actors. (*) marks a change in tense, i.e from 'was'/'were' to 'are'.*

Visuals: 'CALIFORNIA (1850)'

MAN (*Twenties.*)   'No Black, Mulatto person or Indian, shall
be allowed to give evidence in favour of, or
against a white man.'

WOMAN (*Thirties.*)   'Black citizens are prohibited from serving
on juries.' West Virginia.

Text: 'ALABAMA'

SISTER (*Twenty.*)   'No person or corporation shall require
any white female nurse to nurse in wards
or rooms in hospitals, either public or
private, in which Negro men are placed.'

BROTHER
  (*Eighteen.*)   'It shall be unlawful to conduct a
restaurant or other place for the serving of
food in the city, at which white and colored
people are served in the same room.'

MOM   'Unless such white and colored persons are
effectually separated by a solid partition
extending from the floor upward to a
distance of seven feet or higher.'

BROTHER   'And unless a separate entrance from the
street is provided for each compartment.'

GIRL CHILD
  (*Eleven.*)   'All persons licensed to conduct a
restaurant, shall serve either white people

exclusively or colored people exclusively and shall not sell to the two races within the same room or serve the two races anywhere under the same license.' Georgia.

WIFE (*Thirties.*) 'It shall be unlawful for a Negro and white person to play together or in company with each other at any game of pool or billiards.' Alabama.

HUSBAND (*Thirties.*) 'It shall be unlawful for a Negro and white person to play together or in company with each other in any game of cards, dice, dominoes or checkers.' Albama, 1930.

MALE (*Sixties.*) 'All circuses, shows, and tent exhibitions to which the attendance of… more than one race is invited or expected to attend shall provide for the convenience of its patrons not less than two ticket offices with individual ticket sellers, and not less than two entrances to the said performance, with individual ticket takers and receivers, and in the case of outside or tent performances, the said ticket offices shall not be less than twenty-five feet apart.' Louisiana.

Text: 'GEORGIA'

FEMALE (*Twenties.*) 'It shall be unlawful for any amateur white baseball team to play baseball on any vacant lot or baseball diamond within two blocks of a playground devoted to the Negro race, and it shall be unlawful for any amateur Colored baseball team to play baseball in any vacant lot or baseball diamond within two blocks of any playground devoted to the white race.'

OLDER MAN (*Seventies.*) 'The commission shall have the right to make segregation of the white and colored races as to the exercise of rights of fishing, boating and bathing.' Oklahoma.

FEMALE FRIEND 1 (*Twenties*.)	'Every person operating any public hall, theatre – '
MALE FRIEND 2 (*Twenties*.)	' – opera house, motion-picture show or any place of public entertainment – '
FEMALE FRIEND 1	' – or public assemblage which is attended by both white and colored persons – '
MALE FRIEND 2	' – shall separate the white race and the colored race and shall set apart and designate – '
FEMALE FRIEND 1	'– certain seats therin to be occupied by white persons and a portion thereof, or certain seats therein, to be occupied by colored persons.'
MALE FRIEND 2	Virginia.

Text: 'GEORGIA'

GIRLFRIEND 1 (*Forties*.)	'It shall be unlawful for colored people to frequent any park owned or main'tained by the city for the benefit, use and employment of white persons… and unlawful for any white person to frequent any park owned or main'tained by the city for the use and benefit of colored persons.'
GIRLFRIEND 2 (*Forties*.)	'All public parks, recreation centers, playgrounds, etc., are (*) required to be segregated.' 1956. Kentucky.
GIRLFRIEND 1	1950. 'Separate facilities required for white and Black citizens in state parks.' Texas.
MALE TEENAGER (*Eighteen*.)	'All businesses are (*) prohibited from permitting any dancing, social functions, entertainments, athletic training, games, sports or contests on their premises in which the participants are members of the white and African American races.' Kentucky.

Text: 'GEORGIA'

BOYFRIEND 1 (*Thirties*.)	'All persons licensed to conduct the business of selling beer or wine… shall serve either white people exclusively or colored people exclusively and shall not sell to the two races within the same room at any time.'
BOYFRIEND 2 (*Thirties*.)	'It is (*) unlawful for whites and blacks to purchase and consume alcohol on the same location. Punishable (*) by a fine from fifty to five hundred dollars or an imprisonment in the parish prison or jail for up to two years.'
BOY CHILD (*Twelve*.)	'No colored barber shall serve as a barber [to] white women or girls.'
MOM (*Fifties*.)	'Mental Hospitals: In no case shall Negroes and white persons be together.' Georgia. 'The Blind: The board of trustees shall… main'tain a separate building… on separate ground for the admission, care, instruction, and support of all blind persons of the Colored or Black race.' Louisiana. 'Hospital Entrances: There shall be main'tained by the governing authorities of every hospital main'tained by the state for treatment of white and Colored patients separate entrances for white and Colored patients and visitors, and such entrances shall be used by the race only for which they are prepared.' Mississippi. 1909.
	'An institution for the education of colored deaf mutes is (*) to be established. But segregation in this school is (*) still to be enforced.' Kentucky.
DAD (*Fifties*.)	1948. 'The law does(*) not allow African American physicians and nurses to take postgraduate courses in public hospitals…' Kentucky.

1955 Tennessee. 'Separate buildings for Black and white patients in hospitals for the insane.'

Text: 'NORTH CAROLINA'

BROTHER 1 (*Fourteen.*)	'Books shall not be interchangeable between white and colored schools, but shall continue to be used by the race first using them.'
SISTER (*Sixteen.*)	1919... 'Negroes are (*) to use separate branches of county free libraries.' 1925... 'Separate branches for Negroes to be administered by a Negro custodian in all county libraries.' Texas.
BROTHER 2 (*Twenty.*)	1928... 'Separate textbooks for white and African American children.' Kentucky. 1957. 'There are (*) to be no state funds to non-segregated schools.'
WOMAN (*Thirties.*)	'Separate schools can (*) be provided for colored children when there are (*) fifteen or more Colored children within any school district.' Wyoming.
FEMALE TEEN (*Eighteen.*)	'No separate school is (*) allowed to be located within one mile of a separate white school. In cities and towns (*) schools in those areas not within six hundred feet of each other.' Kentucky.
MAN (*Twenty.*)	'The children of white and Colored races committed to the houses of reform shall be kept entirely separate from each other.' Kentucky. The warden shall see that the white convicts shall have separate apartments for both eating and sleeping from the Negro convicts.' Mississippi.
OLDER WOMAN (*Seventies.*)	'It shall be unlawful for any white prisoner to be handcuffed or otherwise

chained or tied to a Negro prisoner.'
Arkansas, 1903.

Text: 'FLORIDA'

MAN (*Thirties.*)   'There shall be separate buildings. Not
nearer than one-fourth mile to each other,
one for white boys and one for Negro boys.
White boys and Negro boys shall not, in
any manner, be associated together or
worked together.'

SISTER 1 (*Forties*)   'Separate washrooms in mines required.'
1955. Tennessee.

SISTER 2 (*Forties*)   'The baths and lockers for the Negroes
shall be separate from the white race, but
may be in the same building.' Oklahoma.

SISTER 1 (*Forties*)   'Employment: In addition, separate rooms
to eat in as well as separate eating and
drinking utensils are (*) required to be
provided for members of white and African
American races.' 1956. Kentucky.

TEENAGER: 'Blacks are (*) not allowed to use the same
hearse as whites.' Oklahoma.

FEMALE TEEN   'The officer in charge shall not bury, or
allow to be buried, any Colored persons
upon ground set apart or used for the burial
of white persons.' Georgia.

Scene Two

UK.

*Filmed: The following are excerpts from slave codes, British
(Jamaican) codes and a few French codes. To be spoken direct to
camera. Various Caucasian UK actors/non-actors. (*) marks an
excerpt from a French code.*

SON (*Twelve*.)	'From the first day of March, no Negro or other slave in this island shall purchase or buy any horse, mare, mule, ass or gelding.'
DAD	'No Negro or other slave shall be allowed to hunt any cattle, horses, mares, mules or asses, in any part of this island with lances, guns, cutlasses or other instruments of death unless in the company of his master, overseer or some other white person, or by permission in writing.'
GRANDDAD	'That any Negro or slave shall fraudulently have in their possession, unknown to his or her master, owner or overseer, any fresh beef, veal, mutton or goat, or the flesh of horse, mare, mule or ass, in any quantity exceeding five and not exceeding twenty pounds weight, such Negro or other slave shall be whipped in such manner as magistrates shall direct.
GRANDDAUGHTER	We forbid slaves from selling sugar cane, for whatever reason or occasion... at the risk of a whipping for the slaves... We also forbid slaves from selling any type of commodities, even fruit, vegetables, firewood, herbs for cooking and animals either at the market, or at individual houses,

without a letter or a known mark from their
masters granting express permission.' (*)

MALE TEENAGER   'That if any Negro or other slave shall,
(*Fourteen*.)   after the first day of January, steal any such
                  horned cattle, sheep, goat, horse, mare,
                  mule or ass – '

HIS MUM   ' – or shall kill any such horned cattle,
(*Forties*.)   sheep, goat, horse, mule or ass
                  with intent to steal the whole carcass or
                  any part of the flesh thereof,
                  such Negro or slave shall on conviction
                  thereof suffer death.'

GIRL CHILD (*Ten*.)   'That in all cases where the punishment of
                      death is inflicted, the execution shall be
                      performed in a public part of the parish – '

HER DAD (*Thirties*.)   ' – care shall be taken by the jailer that the
                        criminal is free from intoxication and the
                        mode of such execution shall be hanging
                        by the neck.'

OLDER MAN   'No slave shall be permitted on any day –
(*Sixties, husband*.)   Sunday excepted – to go out of his or her
                        master's plantation, or to travel from one
                        place to another.'

OLDER WOMAN   'Unless such slave shall have a ticket from
(*Sixties, wife*.)   their master, owner, employer or overseer
                     expressing the time of such slaves setting
                     out, where he or she is going and the time
                     limited for his or her return.'

YOUNG WOMAN   'From the first day of March any slaves
(*Twenties*.)   found at the distance of eight miles from
                  the house or plantation to which he, she or
                  they belong without a ticket to pass shall
                  be deemed a runaway.'

OLDER WOMAN   'Without such, all and every such slave or
                  slaves shall be apprehended and committed
                  to jail,
                  and there be whipped.'

MALE FRIEND 1   'Any free Negro
(*Twenties*.)   free Mulattoes
                       or Indians
                       granting runaway slaves a ticket shall be
                       guilty of forgery,
                       tried
                       and on conviction shall suffer their loss of
                       freedom.'

MALE FRIEND 2   'Where many runaway slaves travel the
(*Twenties*.)   country with false or forged tickets; to
                       prevent such evil practices…
                       all tickets
                       shall be signed by the clerk of the vestry of
                       the parish where such persons shall
                       reside – '

MALE FRIEND 1   ' – or
                       by either of the church wardens of said
                       parish.'

GIRLFRIEND 1   '(That) any person who shall apprehend
(*Forties*.)   such runaways (will) be entitled to receive
                       from the owner, overseer or manager of
                       such slave the sum of ten shillings and no
                       more, besides mile money – at the rate of
                       one shilling per mile for the first five miles
                       and six pence per mile afterwards.'

GIRLFRIEND 2   'If any slave or slaves sentenced to hard
(*Forties*.)   labour or life wilfully runs away or escapes
                       from the workhouse – upon capture and
                       conviction such slaves
                       are punishable by death.'

GRANDAD   'The fugitive slave who has been on the
                       run for one month from the day his master
                       reported him to the police,
                       shall have his ears cut off and shall be
                       branded… on one shoulder.
                       If he commits the same infraction for
                       another month,
                       again counting from the day he is reported,

he shall have his hamstring cut
and be branded...
on the other shoulder.
The third time
he shall be put to death.' (*)

BOYFRIEND 1   '...all means and opportunities of slaves
(*Thirties.*)   committing rebellious conspiracies and
                     other crimes to the ruin and destruction of
                     white people are to be prevented
                     and that proper punishments should be
                     appointed for all crimes to be by them
                     committed.'

BOYFRIEND 2   'And be it further enacted that if any free
(*Thirties.*)   Negro
                     Mulatto
                     or Indian
                     knowingly allows unlawful assemblies of
                     slaves at his or her house or settlements
                     such
                     free Negro
                     Mulatto
                     or Indian
                     shall suffer six months' imprisonment.'

SISTER 1 (*Twenty.*)   'No master – '

SISTER 2 (*Twenty.*)   ' – or owner – '

SISTER 1   ' – shall allow slaves to assemble together
                     and to beat their military drums – '

SISTER 2   ' – or blow their horns – '

SISTER 1   ' – or blow their shells upon any plantation,
                     pen or settlement – '

SISTER 2   ' – or – '

SISTER 1   ' – in any yard or place under his or their
                     care or management.'

SISTER 2   '(In the same way) we forbid slaves
                     belonging to different masters to gather in
                     the day or night

whether claiming for wedding or otherwise,
whether on their master's property or
elsewhere,
and still less in the main roads or faraway
places, on pain of corporal punishment
which shall not be less than the whip and
branding...
...and which cases of frequent violations...
can be punished with death.' (*)

WOMAN 2 (*Seventies*.)   'We forbid slaves to carry any weapon, or
large sticks on pain of whipping and of
confiscation of the weapon to the profit of
those who seize them.' (*)

GIRL CHILD   'The masters may also, when they believe
that their slaves so deserve, chain them and
have them beaten with rods or straps...'(*)

WIFE (*Thirties*.)   'If any Negro or slave whatsoever shall
offer any violence to any Christian by
striking or the like,
such Negro or slave shall
for his or her first offence
be severely whipped by the constable.

HUSBAND (*Thirties*.)   For his second offence of that nature
he shall be severely whipped,
his nose slit,
and be burned in some part of his face with
a hot iron.'

CHILD (*Nine*.)   'If any slave shall offer any violence
by striking or otherwise to any white
person,
such slave shall be confined to hard labour
for life,
or punished with death.'

CHILD 2   'The slave who has struck his master in
the face or has drawn blood, or has
similarly struck the wife of his master, his
mistress, or their children,
shall be punished by death...' (*)

CHILD'S MUM
(*Forties.*)

'…Several slaves have lately found
means to desert from their owners and
depart from this island,
to the great damage of such owners,
(and) in evil example to other slaves who
may be induced to attempt to conspire to
do the same.

CHILD'S DAD
(*Forties.*)

From and after the first day of March,
if any slave shall run away
and go off
or
conspire
or
attempt to go off
this island
in any ship, boat, canoe
or
other vessel
or be
aiding
abetting
or affiliating to any such slaves
he, she or they
shall suffer such punishments…

including death.'

Epilogue

Y. ADULT (US)   Gimme one reason to not.

ADULT

Y. WOMAN (US)   Go on.

MAN (UK)   Go on.

ADULT

Y. WOMAN (US)   Give me one reason to not.

                  END.

A Nick Hern Book

ear for eye first published in Great Britain in 2018 as a paperback original by Nick
Hern Books Limited, The Glasshouse, 49a Goldhawk Road, London W12 8QP,
in association with the Royal Court Theatre

ear for eye copyright © 2018 debbie tucker green

debbie tucker green has asserted her right to be identified as the author of
this work

Cover image: Root

Designed and typeset by Nick Hern Books, London
Printed and bound in Great Britain by Mimeo UK Ltd

A CIP catalogue record for this book is available from the British Library

ISBN 978 1 84842 762 4